AP Huh

*Curriculum conversations with
alternative provision leaders*

Mary Myatt and John Tomsett

Cover design by Madeleine Miller

JOHN CATT
FROM HODDER EDUCATION

Orders: please contact Hachette UK Distribution, Hely Hutchinson Centre, Milton Road, Didcot, Oxfordshire, OX11 7HH. Telephone: +44 (0)1235 827827. Email education@hachette.co.uk. Lines are open from 9 a.m. to 5 p.m., Monday to Friday.

ISBN: 9781036004187

© Mary Myatt and John Tomsett 2024

First published in 2024 by
John Catt from Hodder Education,
An Hachette UK Company
15 Riduna Park, Station Road,
Melton, Woodbridge IP12 1QT
Telephone: +44 (0)1394 389850

www.johncatt.com

MIX
Paper | Supporting
responsible forestry
FSC
www.fsc.org   FSC™ C104740

Testimonials

There is so much brilliant practice in our schools which goes unheralded and unshared. This is why the *Huh* series of books on the curriculum is so important – Myatt and Tomsett have given a platform to colleagues across the school system who are doing great work that needs to be heard far and wide. *AP Huh* brings together voices who are working at the sharp end of things, picking up children who, for one reason or another, cannot access mainstream education. It is a book of deep hope. Our colleagues working in AP are extraordinary and their stories recounted here in these curriculum conversations are inspiring.

Jonny Uttley
CEO, The Education Alliance Trust

AP Huh is a fabulous collection of insights into the vital role that AP plays in the education of some of our most vulnerable young children. The experiences of the excellent contributors are insightful and inspiring. The interview format of the book draws you in and makes this such an easy and pleasurable read. As the headteacher of a mainstream secondary school, I have learned so much from this fabulous book. It would not be an exaggeration to say that my thinking has been transformed. A must-read for anyone who is serious about achieving genuine inclusion!

Patrick Cozier
Headteacher, Highgate Wood School and Sixth Form Centre

As a reader who has cerebral palsy and talks about my mainstream education, I have read a number of books and articles on inclusive practices and SEND provision, but this book is the most informative that I ever read on inclusive education. I took a lot from *AP Huh*. This will definitely be useful for new and current educational professionals. I particularly enjoyed reading some of the stories from the contributors about their experiences in education and how they got into teaching and alternative provision. By the sounds of it, they are amazing and are making a positive difference!

Ellise Hollie Hayward
Motivational/public speaker, disabilities correspondent,
inclusion and AAC ambassador

Alternative provision provides safety, learning, friendship and hope for our most vulnerable children. The very best alternative provision is wonderfully ambitious and inclusive; but it can so often go wrong, putting children's futures at risk. *AP Huh* is an energising read, continuing the *Huh* series into possibly the most overlooked and underrated territory. To read through these conversations, or even just to dip in, is illuminating, educational, moving and invaluable. We are at a time when the number of persistent absentees in our schools is growing exponentially. Society can ill afford to ignore these children and the places in which they can learn and be successful.

Keziah Featherstone
Executive headteacher, Q3 Academy Tipton

I've always believed that the best CPD is simply talking to other teachers. *AP Huh* is exactly that! A series of engaging, succinct and informative conversations with current teachers/school leaders about the intricacies of AP curriculum. It offers practical advice and guidance in a user-friendly format. There is so much to take away! Essential reading for all stakeholders in alternative provision.

Omar Akbar
Teacher of science and education author

Welcome to a journey that promises to transform the way we think about education in alternative provision. The authors, drawing upon a wealth of experience, present a vision of education where every student is seen, heard and valued. *AP Huh* is not just about the 'what' and 'how' of curriculum design; it is profoundly about the 'why'. It challenges us to rethink the purpose of education in alternative provision, advocating for a curriculum that fosters resilience, creativity and a lifelong love of learning.

Wasim Butt
Director of AP and special academies, Ormiston Academies Trust

Teachers up and down the country are saying that behaviour has been more challenging since COVID. Therefore, *AP Huh* could not have come soon enough. It is a chance to learn from the absolute experts working in alternative provision, who are making an incredible difference in challenging circumstances, supporting the pupils who need help the most. Like other *Huh* books, the interview format, impeccably facilitated by Mary Myatt and John Tomsett, gives real practitioners a voice. AP teachers often don't control the narrative, and I learned so much from hearing their words about their work. What shines through strongly is the proper power of relationships and the importance of giving students something to be proud of through their curriculum. This book is essential reading for all mainstream teachers and leaders. We have never needed it more.

Haili Hughes
Senior lecturer at the University of Sunderland
and head of education at IRIS Connect

AP Huh is an excellent read, full of insights and wisdom from practising alternative provision leaders. The in-conversation style unpacks each leader's curriculum journey and decision making, illustrating practical ways to improve outcomes for students in alternative provision.

Shaun Brown
Programmes director, The Difference

Leaders in *AP Huh* discuss the unique perspectives of children on the outside of education, isolated from school and their peers. It is often a sense of belonging that they are missing; as Jess Mahdavi-Gladwell notes, these children look for safety beyond home. Historically, some of these young people might have been considered 'uneducable', as John d'Abbro explains; his unique perspective shows they were most likely unheard or misunderstood. *AP Huh* is that conversation you may have always wanted with a leader in AP, so that you can better understand students missing from our registers. It poses the question for all of us in mainstream education: how can we consciously do better, both for our colleagues and our pupils in AP?

Ms Mabina Ahmed
Head of science, Prendergast Vale School

In this book, Mary Myatt and John Tomsett expertly bring together some of the most forward thinking and innovative leaders working in alternative provision today. Through a series of 'curriculum conversations', key themes and practices are revealed, lifting the veil on what happens behind the often perceived-to-be closed doors of alternative provision. *AP Huh* is a must-read for all teachers and leaders working in AP who want to learn more about how common challenges are addressed by colleagues across the sector and in different settings. Most importantly, this is an essential read for teachers and leaders working in mainstream schools who frequently feel that the practice of AP colleagues is shrouded in mystery.

Eleanor Bernardes
Strategic lead for the APSEND National MAT CEOs network

Acknowledgements

The first 'thank you' goes to all those colleagues working and learning in the alternative provision sector who volunteered their time to speak to us about their work. It has been a genuine privilege to engage in those conversations and to learn about how they develop the curriculum for children whose needs aren't being met in mainstream provision. It has been both illuminating and humbling in equal measure; the *Huh* project has been a learning experience for us both, and it is fair to say we have learned a huge amount from the interviews that comprise this latest and final book in the series. Next, a special 'thank you' goes to Bennie Kara for her foreword, which provides an insightful opening to *AP Huh*. Finally, we would like to thank Fran Myatt who continues to be the operational genius behind our work, Natasha Gladwell who has proofread each chapter with incredible accuracy and efficiency, and Alex at John Catt for supporting the *Huh* project without equivocation.

John: For Lloyd Brown, my dear friend, and one of the most dedicated, kindest, expert educators of children in challenging circumstances I know.

Mary: For Loic Menzies, always an advocate for young people on the margins.

Contents

Introduction

Mary Myatt, April 2024

Being human is tough. Being a young person in difficult circumstances is tougher. While young people in alternative provision have moved from their mainstream setting, it's important that their dignity is preserved in the process. One of the characteristics of our conversations with colleagues working in alternative provision is that this is front and centre of their thinking. For example, in many contexts, alternative provision is framed as a 'fresh start' rather than a last resort. This is an important distinction because it emphasises hope and expectation that each young person has the potential to thrive.

We also found that the curriculum in these settings is focused initially on preparation for learning, hence a strong focus on personal development and, in most cases, reintegration to the pupil's home school is a priority. The culture and ways of working both for adults and young people is intentionally framed and enacted. One example of this is the extensive use of coaching both for young people and the professionals working with them.

There were some remarkable insights from this work: for example, Cath Kitchen, chair of the National Association for Hospital Education, told us that there are no national data for the number of pupils receiving hospital education. While this population of young people is mobile and across different settings, the lack of national data has implications for funding and for meeting the needs of this vulnerable group at a national level.

One of the joys of these conversations is that colleagues doing deep work in different contexts have a way of framing their thinking that is super helpful for those of us trying to find out more about the business of supporting young people to get back on track. In one context, the curriculum is framed as a bus journey compared to an aeroplane journey in mainstream, where there is a clear 'flightpath' through the curriculum. In an alternative provision setting, pupils might have one or more 'stops' before returning to mainstream. This means that the journey between the stops needs to be appropriate, rich and have the capacity for pupils to secure elements of the curriculum that are likely to set them up for success when they move on.

It has been a privilege to spend time talking with colleagues who are putting their hearts and intellects into making alternative provision a great deal for their young people. We all have something to learn from them.

John Tomsett, April 2024

Several strands of thinking emerged as we conducted the interviews for *AP Huh*. The importance of celebrating the success of pupils in AP was emphasised repeatedly. As John d'Abbro pointed out, 'Many of these youngsters have experienced what Hargreaves would call "the destruction of their dignity",' and rebuilding their dignity begins with celebrating success – *any* success. Indeed, Eugene Dwaah insists that his colleagues celebrate 'every little success, even if it's the minutest thing'.

The most important success for many pupils in AP is success in English and mathematics. Providers are clear that good levels of literacy and numeracy provide the foundations for everything else in the AP curriculum. There are some remarkable personal stories in this book. John d'Abbro's account of his own struggle to read left us all in tears, and erstwhile army officer Neil Miller's experience helping his soldiers read and write is remarkable.

While the emphasis upon the core subjects in AP is similar to mainstream, there are crucial differences. The advantages of small classes and low teacher–pupil ratios are highlighted several times in the book. The children being educated in AP require a great deal of flexibility. Initially, their main need is often social and emotional. Until the children are ready to learn emotionally, there seems little point in insisting they engage in the academic. Small, flexible organisations like the ones featured in *AP Huh* can provide the environments the children need. Mainstream is not for every child, as Jess Mahdavi-Gladwell so brilliantly points out in her pithy aphorism, 'It's *main*-stream, not *all*-stream.'

Beyond SEMH, there is a complex relationship between AP and SEND provision. They are often conflated. When we interviewed people for the *SEND Huh* book, we were clearly talking about SEND and not about alternative provision. But when we interviewed colleagues about AP, there was suddenly an overlap. In several interviews, it is clear that the needs of young people are being met in diverse ways. And with growing numbers of children requiring provision different to the mainstream, many schools are beginning to set up alternative provision *within* mainstream settings.

A final thought. In his book *We-Think*, Charlie Leadbeater writes about the impact the internet was having on the mainstream media. He saw the BBC and other huge media 'boulders' being undermined and, ultimately, changed forever by the world wide web, where 'pebble' platforms like YouTube were encouraging 'mass creativity and innovation'. No one had to pitch their ideas to a TV executive any longer; they could just upload their work for the whole world to see.

I recall Leadbeater's metaphor because I have a hunch a similar process might just be happening to the school system. The big boulders of education – mainstream schools – are being forced to rethink their role. The pandemic altered the social contract between home and school. To increasing numbers of parents, the requirement for their children to attend school no longer seems to be the unquestioned imperative it once was. And the increasingly sophisticated online curriculum provision engendered by the mass closure of schools during the COVID crisis means that children can now learn from home in a meaningful way.

Indeed, some children with autism spectrum condition truly loved the lockdown and learning online. They didn't have to contend with the busyness and unpredictability of a school, with its numerous, random human interactions. They loved the regularity of their day. And the megatrend towards increasing individualisation suggests that the demand from growing numbers of individual children for their individual educational needs to be met will only continue to grow.

The UK Parliament's Research Briefing published in December 2023 admitted that no one knows how many children are being home-schooled in this country. Estimates are just shy of 100,000 children. That is more than 100 average-sized secondary schools; 100 educational 'boulders' that have been shattered into 100,000 individuals with unique needs. Eugene Dwaah's Evolution Education is one of many pebble-sized organisations helping meet those needs. What I learned from the experts we interviewed for *AP Huh* tells me we'll need many more Evolution Educations in the future.

Foreword

On reading *AP Huh*, I am struck by the sheer commitment the alternative provision community demonstrates to the young people in its care. Whether that is catering for medical or SEND needs, for SEMH needs or providing a fresh start so that those children have a fighting chance to go on to be the best they can be, AP is truly remarkable. This book is important. The ideas and experiences articulated here show us two things: that children are not 'cookie-cutter' beings, but complex individuals and that AP educators are wholly dedicated to ensuring that each child has an education that they deserve.

Certain themes emerge across the chapters. We hear often about adapting the curriculum so that children can learn at a pace and in a style that suits them in the moment or in the long term. What stands out is the need to show that the curriculum matters; it is a vehicle for future success, and it sits alongside the incredible pastoral work that is carefully and cleverly woven into each day. This readiness to adapt is key; it doesn't allow for 'dumbing down' or 'lowering expectations', but is central to providing an excellent education while explicitly noticing the individual being educated. What is refreshing, and perhaps provides an insight into personalising education, is how much the curriculum spends time on preparing young people to learn before they embark on qualifications that will serve them in the future.

The leaders, parents and young people interviewed show us that there might be another way. All educators can learn vital lessons about treating young people as individuals, with individual needs, first. Yes, there is recognition of the need to have qualifications in mathematics or English, but that recognition includes an unpicking as to why some students struggle to access those subjects. And there is understanding, not blame.

What is the result? Firstly, children who *attend* their AP settings. A number of times throughout the book's chapters, we see attendance reporting at 95% or 98%. This is no surprise. When a child or young person feels understood, is given time to catch up, is allowed to be themselves and to make choices, we see engagement. Perhaps it is more than personalisation at play here. Debra Rutley says: 'I talk about love all the time, and particularly in our AP settings, because sometimes children present themselves as "unlovable". They are the ones who need our love the most. I will say to staff, "Is that good enough for my child? Are we treating them with love? Because they are going to learn with and through love."'

Flexibility in designing provision emerges as a theme, and always with the child at the heart of the thinking. There are frequent questions about how much time should be spent on each subject, about suitability of courses of study in the moment, and about how subjects can be a stepping stone to the next stages of a young person's life.

It is heartening to see how many extracurricular options are woven into a young person's experience in AP. From trips and visits to pop-up science labs, there is a wealth of opportunity. We often talk about the need for children to experience the world. What is happening in AP shows that collaboration with carefully selected external organisations is hugely important in delivering those experiences. We hear about Jamie's Farm, First Story, intergenerational meetings, celebrations of Black history and much more. It is the richness and fullness of experience in an educational setting that provides not only knowledge, but relational awareness, confidence and recognition.

Crucially, whether a young person can – or should – be reintegrated into mainstream education is a constant issue. AP is both a respite and a mechanism for inclusion; not a last resort, but a safety net. The concept of returning to a 'home school' recurs in the accounts in the book. In all cases, the interviewees tell us time and time again that collaboration with the 'home school' is essential and that transition is managed with communication with parents/carers and with the school, encompassing what they have achieved in their studies and how they will continue to thrive.

I am struck by the innovation and imagination of hospital schools in particular. The agility needed to provide schooling for those regularly in and out of hospital is evident in the way that teams of staff work with casual and long-term admissions. Compassion, high expectations and agility combine beautifully to make sure that those with medical needs have the best experience they can have. As Stephen Deadman, headteacher of Leicester Children's Hospital School, says: 'It's not sticking rigidly to your plan. It's being flexible within that lesson as well when the health needs are not right. Sometimes, what that child needs – when they're deeply upset because they're worried or they're in pain – is someone just to talk to and to have a story read to them. It's having the emotional intelligence to recognise that.' It is remarkable that there is no data telling us how many children have received education in a hospital setting. If the accounts in this book are anything to go by, those children are receiving the best care they can under difficult circumstances.

Of all of the stories featured in the book, I am particularly drawn to Izzy's story of home education with her mum because it centres on a child's experience of education. It reminds us that for some children, home education is a necessary move that works for them. It also reminds us of all the people who take responsibility for a child's education: parents and carers, teaching assistants, teachers and leaders in settings that are designed to ensure no child is left behind. This book is a remarkable testament to their hard work.

Bennie Kara

It's personal...

A conversation with John d'Abbro

For 28 years, John d'Abbro was headteacher of the New Rush Hall Group, an organisation working with children experiencing social, emotional and/or mental health difficulties. The group consisted of an all-age day special school, three pupil referral units, an adolescent psychiatric unit, an outreach team and an Early Years provision. He is a nationally renowned source of expertise in working with children in alternative provision.

Great to be speaking with you, John. Please tell us a little about your teaching career.

Actually, I had a spell in the early 1970s as a student in AP! I had a bit of a chequered school career. So, I am a poacher turned gamekeeper. I eventually went on to train as a teacher. I worked initially in mainstream and wasn't much good at it. I knew I had something to offer so I went to work in a school for children who were, in those days, labelled *educationally subnormal* or ESN, God forbid! Then I went to work in a residential school for children who were *maladjusted*.

We had a *remedial* class when I went to secondary school in 1975...

It's hard to believe the language that was used back then... the social construction of disability. That was in a residential school in Surrey, but we would send kids home at weekends, and a lot of what was happening just didn't make sense to me. So, I left that place and went to work in a school in Somerset, which was, in all but name, an AP. And after two years, I got the headship. And then I ran that for four years. With hindsight, I think it must've been okay because Lord Elton and his people interviewed me for *The Elton Report* (1989).

I think, because of my own chequered school career, I had an affinity with the work, and I used to get on quite well with kids. I wasn't a great academic, but I think I understood what was needed. We designed quite a unique and bespoke curriculum in those days. I wrote a chapter in a book about it 35-odd years ago, and I reread it this afternoon just to get up to speed for our conversation. And it's amazing that many of the things that I was advocating in that chapter – and subsequently in the work I've done in the last 30-odd years running a soft federation that contained three pupil referral units – many of those things I still believe. We ran a four-term year, for instance. I think a four-term year is much more logical, much more coherent. It made it much easier for us to be modular because it meant we had four 10-week terms. We never went more than five weeks without a break. So, the kids and staff were less stressed. And, interestingly, crime rates were lower for the youngsters. The family relationships at home were better and attainment was better. That to me is the start of the curriculum. For youngsters in AP – as it should be in all schools, but I think particularly in AP – the curriculum has to be more student-focused. So, I did that at Sedgemoor in Bridgwater, and then I was going to leave teaching, believe it or not, and run an Italian restaurant like my father and my brother had done – my cultural roots are Italian – but I saw this job advertised in Redbridge, which I thought I'd never get, because I was still relatively young. I was 34 and I thought it was a huge job. But I applied for it, and I got it! And, you know, that became the New Rush Hall Group, which was, for the time, quite cutting edge for youngsters who presented challenging behaviour – a term I prefer to ones like SEMH, SEBD, maladjusted and EBD.

Although I always tried to keep a teaching role, what I think I did was became a strategic manager; I became – I don't like the term – the executive head. And it was like seven service centres, which included an adolescent psychiatric unit, an all-age special school, an outreach team, an Early Years provision and three PRUs. And I led and managed them.

AP has always been one of my favourite places to work because you've got all the good things about a school, but you can also get rid of some of the bits that you don't like about a school. If you start to develop a curriculum, at KS3 and KS4, you need to get the students on board. I think the notion of offering them more flexible working practices is a good starting point. So, I did all that work with children who presented challenging behaviours, and I think we did a good job. We did some really good work.

We need to talk a bit differently about primary and secondary – most of my experience and expertise is in secondary – but I think the starting point is that the curriculum must be a bit alternative, and it has to be compensatory. Many of these youngsters have experienced what David Hargreaves would call 'the destruction of their dignity'. I think we must recognise in curriculum design that many youngsters end up in PRUs because mainstream schools aren't good enough for them. Now, I'm not knocking mainstream schools, but mainstream is not the gold standard for all youngsters, particularly those who've lost the love of learning, who can't manage their own behaviour appropriately at times – they need something different. And I think just trying to give them what they've already had, which hasn't worked, is a no-no.

I'm ambivalent about whether we should have APs in primary. And I know that'll upset some people, which is not to say there aren't some outstanding ones out there. I currently work in the DfE Behaviour Hubs programme as an advisor. There are some fantastic primary PRUs. I think because the good ones are so good, perhaps I'm changing my view on whether we should have primary PRUs. For me, AP is different to PRUs, remember. AP is more of an amorphous term, and it covers a wider range of provision. I do think at KS3, we should get kids in, sort them out, and get shot of them. And I don't mean that in a rude way. I think that many youngsters' best life chances are in mainstream school. Having said that, I think at the back end of Year 9, when youngsters have realised that the mainstream curriculum is not going to afford them what they need to be successful as they move into KS4 and KS5, I think PRUs can be highly effective.

The PRUs that we ran made a commitment to students which went something like, 'We'll take you through the duration for the next two years and we'll give you an alternative and compensatory curriculum, which will have elements of the national curriculum. It will also have some bespoke stuff that recognises that you need to learn how to behave. You need to learn how to be more sociable. You need to find out what it is that's going to make you become re-enfranchised through learning.' And so, I'm a real advocate for getting the basics right. And I have openly incentivised children throughout my career by saying things like, 'If you get a reading age of 10, the school will give you an iPod Shuffle.' I remember a minister visiting one day and saying, 'You know, you're bribing kids.' I said, 'Absolutely, I've got no problem with that.' What I know is, a child's chance of going to prison decreases massively if they've got a reading age of 10. And once you've got a reading age of 10, you can then start saying to kids that we can coach them into getting GCSEs or some of the other qualifications.

So, beyond blatant bribery, when it comes to curriculum design in AP, what are your thoughts?!

I believe that education saved me, and I believe you do kids a disservice if you don't do the basics. So, in any curriculum I would design, English and maths would be at the core of it. Then I would have preparation for parenthood, life skills and social skills, job preparation, and supportive self-study. I used to teach children how to study and say to them, 'Look, once you can learn how to study, then the world's your oyster, because once we have taught you how to read and you can do your basic maths, you can then pick the things to learn that really interest you.' You know, I've worked with some really disturbed and disturbing youngsters, but made them sense the progress they were making, which made them feel better about themselves and get re-enfranchised back into the learning process. So, I'm quite traditional. In the morning should be what I call 'heads down' subjects. And then the afternoon I think should be more vocational subjects, including things like a leavers' programme, which would include things like preparation for parenthood and money management.

This is what the curriculum looked like back in the 1980s in Bridgwater at the PRU I led, and I would keep the vast majority of it today:

Terms 1 and 4	9.15-9.30	9.30-10.15	10.20-11.00	11.15-12.15	1.00-2.15	2.30-3.30
MONDAY	Prefect tutor group Joint tutor group	5th Year: Maths	English	Social skills	Woodwork	Snooker
					Motorbikes	
		4th Year: Maths	English	Home management	Sedgemoor Centre Ltd	
TUESDAY	Tutor group	5th Year: Maths	Humanities	Leavers' programme	Duke of Edinburgh Awards	
		4th Year: Current affairs	Supported self-study	Science projects	Pop videos	
WEDNESDAY	Tutor group	5th Year: Maths	Preparation for parenthood	Home management	Swimming	a) Weight training b) Badminton c) Squash
		5th Year: English	Supported self-study	Money management and introduction to work	Art	Round robin
					Engineering	Engineering
THURSDAY	Tutor group	4th Year: Maths	Integrated studies	Social skills	Skittles and unihoc round robin	Cooking
		5th Year: Work experience practical, work experience coursework, work experience canvassing			Drum workshop	
					Work experience canvassing	
FRIDAY	Joint tutor group	5th Year: Current affairs	Supported self-study	Job preparation	Tutor group	
		4th Year: Preparation for life skills				

Terms 2 and 3	9.15–9.30	9.30–10.15	10.20–11.00	11.15–12.15	1.00–2.15	2.30–3.30
MONDAY	Prefect tutor group	5th Year: Maths	English	Social skills	Engineering	Engineering
	Joint tutor group	4th Year: Maths	English	Home management	Football	Football
TUESDAY	Tutor group	4th Year: Preparation for parenthood	Supported self-study	Science projects	Candid camera	Candid camera
					Swimming	Snooker
		5th Year: Work experience practical, work experience coursework, work experience canvassing, job canvassing				
WEDNESDAY	Tutor group	4th Year: Humanities	English	Life skills	Motorbikes	
		5th Year: Preparation for parenthood	Projects	Job preparation	Art/pottery	
					Drama	
THURSDAY	Tutor group	4th Year: Maths	Current affairs	Social skills	Woodwork	Skittles
					Orienteering	
		5th Year: Work experience practical, work experience coursework, work experience canvassing, job canvassing				
FRIDAY	Joint tutor group	5th Year: Maths	Home management	Leavers' programme	Week 1: Tutor groups	
		4th Year: Current affairs	Integrated studies	Money management	Week 2: Options – Popmobility and cooking	

So, I think an effective curriculum engages the kids. If you're not engaging them, you're not getting it right. When the kids engage, they don't sod about. I learned that quite early on. You might say, 'Oh, John, that's really naive.' But I would honestly say I've lived it and got kids to buy in. The principle is the same when you've got someone who's very gifted in a mainstream school – you've got to find a way of stretching that gifted child so that they feel they are learning and they're reaching their full potential. In the context of an AP, I think it's about applied learning. And I think it has to be different to what they've had before, because what they had didn't work.

In AP you need a curriculum that ameliorates some of the additional needs of children who are in PRUs, APs, adolescent psychiatric centres or special schools, but also re-engages them in learning. At KS3, I want to get shot of them and get them back into mainstream wherever possible and appropriate. And so, the curriculum is effective if I get them back to mainstream school, and they're not disadvantaged by being in the AP. And that's the other big thing. You've got to be at least as good pedagogy-wise in AP as you are in mainstream. And if you're not, then don't call it special or don't call it AP, because that's not fair. You're doing the kids a disservice. You know, they get one chance at being a kid, and one chance at being in the compulsory education system. You've got to be at least as good pedagogically as you are in a mainstream. And for some kids that will mean the full national curriculum. You know, I've worked with some kids in PRUs and we've had to go to our local grammar school and say, 'Look, this kid's so able, take a punt. This kid is gifted. He was in a Catholic school and told the headteacher to f*** off, and guess what? He got permanently excluded. He's got that wrong and he's got to learn the consequences of that. But actually, he doesn't need to be excluded from education for the rest of his life.'

So, some students come to you in AP, and you're saying at certain ages it's right they go back to mainstream school. And at other moments you say they've got to the point where it really hasn't worked, which means they've got to stay in AP. I'm interested in where that cut-off point is.

Okay, so I think you've got to look at every child as an individual. In mainstream, you go from groups to the individual. In AP and special, we go from the individual to groups. Now, some youngsters may not want to go back to mainstream, and they say, 'Look, I'm better off here.' Professor Sally Thomson suggests special schools exist so that mainstream schools can function. Some people won't like that, but that's the reality. If you look historically at why special schools were invented after the 1944 Education Act, it was so that they could take certain children out of the mainstream. It's only since 1974 that *all* children were entitled to be educated. Up until 1974 in this country, we still had a group of people who were known as uneducable. My sister wasn't entitled to education because she had cerebral palsy. Legally, my mum couldn't say, 'My daughter *must* go to school.'

But going back to KS3, I would say as a starting point to kids, 'You've been referred here, you've not been sent.' That's really important ideologically. If you're trying to make someone feel better about themselves, you don't say this is the end of the line. You say, 'You've been referred here, we're good at what we do, we can help you, and you've got to buy in.' And then there's supporting parents and carers and getting it right with them. They have all seen the destruction of their dignity. The parents are often grieving for the child that they didn't have, or that they wanted to have.

Ultimately, with some kids, you would know that you're *not* going to get shot of them at the end of KS3, but you would still have the expectation right up until the last week that they have to go back to mainstream school. The expectations have to be high. I would never run a KS3 and KS4 AP combined. In Redbridge, we had separate KS3 and KS4 PRUs. I don't think you can do the two together, because of contamination – the older kids get into the gangs, they get into more deviant behaviour, and you don't want them teaching the younger kids bad things. The younger kids need a different type of safety, role models and security. Putting them in with the big players is a mistake – and they're not all boys, I mean the girls as well, and girls are more challenging than boys in my experience, particularly in AP.

Another thing I used to say – particularly to KS4 children – was, 'I will never teach you anything you don't need to learn.' I'm a firm advocate of applied learning. And that used to really stretch me. I would always find a way of saying to children, 'Anything we teach you, you're going to need to learn.' And that's quite frightening on one level, because it's quite disabling as a teacher, but from an integrity point of view, it's crucial.

It is important to see children for what they can become rather than how they are behaving in the here and now. It's about re-enfranchising children, saying, 'Look, you might've had a chequered school career, you might not have started off well, but you've still got 18 months and you can turn your life around and make something of it.'

Don't get me wrong. I was quite insistent that children were challenged around their inappropriate behaviour. But it was a carrot-and-stick curriculum. We would do some interesting things like motorbiking. But guess what? You didn't get to do motorbiking unless you completed your maths and your English. And you know, that's a bit fascist-like, but I passionately believe that if you can leave school reading and writing, knowing how to manage your stress, knowing what the implications of having children are, you don't replicate the cycle of deprivation that you may have experienced yourself. And that can be quite punchy and quite challenging.

Beyond the curriculum, what helped you persuade often disaffected young people to engage with their learning?

So, one thing I used to say to children was, 'We can negotiate what you're learning, but it's not negotiable that you will learn. The adults are in charge. You have to come to school. You have to learn. And if you don't learn, then we may not be doing our job properly, so we'll try to support you more. But the bottom line is if you come to one of our PRUs, you will be successful.' And I'm proud of our track record, you know, it really was pretty damned good. And talk about serendipity, I got an email last night from a young woman, a mother now, who I taught 30 years ago, saying, 'I just want to let you know I've now got my PhD, I've got four children, I live in France... and you guys saved my life.' She made me think of the woman who taught me to read. At 15 I was illiterate. It wasn't learning difficulties. I knew I just hadn't made the right connections. I had convinced myself that I couldn't read and write. I had a sister who had cerebral palsy, God bless her. And I think the knock-on effect on us as a family impacted on me. I was always pretty good at getting on with people, doing the shopping, had all the social skills and things, but wasn't particularly academic. And I think that that's why AP has to be compensatory because many of the kids have had poor experiences in mainstream school. That's not to say their behaviour is okay – inappropriate behaviour needs to be challenged because it's not okay – but you need to understand what's behind it. I don't believe most kids come to school with the sole intention of wanting to upset their teachers. I really don't. And that's despite my Catholic upbringing and original sin and all that. I think the human condition wants to be sociable.

I think the human condition has a natural instinct to want to learn. And the skill of people in AP is doing two things. One is saying, 'This is a learning institution, first and foremost. You're going to have to come to school. If you don't have 95% attendance, we're going to be on your case. I'll come and get you out of bed in the morning.' And I've done that. And I would still do that. I think it's completely appropriate. If you show kids you care about them, you're going to walk the talk. The other thing is saying, 'You are going to learn a curriculum where some of what you did in mainstream, *you're still going to have to do*. You need that for life. But we can also tease you into learning again and make it exciting. So, get your behaviour right. Get your English and maths and science to a certain level. And then let's develop your social skills, let's challenge you, let's teach you how to be assertive rather than aggressive.'

Thinking about that woman who's got four kids and a PhD living in France and you and your team saved her life... I want to ask... who saved *you*? There must be a story there too...

I'm welling up... because every time I tell this story, it, you know...

You don't have to...

It's okay...

Okay, well, tell us then...

So, I was really good at football when I was a kid... Catholic England school boys. I always thought I'd be a footballer. My mum ended up being a teacher and a lecturer, and education was important to us. But my family broke up for a while and I lost my way a bit. And I thought, 'Well, I'm going to be a footballer, so I don't need to learn about reading and writing and going to school.' I used to go to school regularly and I did something I shouldn't have done. I tied the headteacher's bumper to a drainpipe and she drove off and ripped the bumper off the back of her car. But that was partly because I'd just been caned because I was rude to the priest. He'd said, 'Let us pray to God' for my mother and father who had just broken up (they subsequently got back together again) and I'm thinking, 'Pray to God? This is the God that's given me a sister who's a spastic' – I don't mean that emotively, that's just the term that we used in those days, and I know we'd use 'cerebral palsy' now – 'I've got a mum and dad who have just broken up, and I'm being caned for being rude to the priest. It doesn't make sense.' So, I was kicked out.

Fortunately, there were two people who were really significant. One was the headteacher of the next school I went to – Jim Rudden – and the other was Phil Edwards who was an educational psychologist. He tested me. He said, 'John, you're not *thick*.' I don't like that word, but that's what they said in those days. The school, Bishop Thomas Grant, provided genuine comprehensive education where you had 28 in a mixed-ability class: 14 of average ability, seven below average and seven above average. It was a comprehensive school where kids were doing Russian and Chinese, *in the 1970s*. And the head believed that if there were six kids that wanted to do an A-level, he'd find a teacher. And it was wonderful, and I couldn't believe it.

I'd gone for the interview at the school and the head rang up the previous head – and I'm in the room with my mum and my sister – and asked her about me and my old head said, 'He's a bully, he's this, and he's that.' I didn't think I was a bully, but she described me as a monster, basically.

And this man, God bless him, Mr Rudden, with a brilliant piece of psychology, turned around to me and said, 'Well, what do you think about that?' I replied, 'It's not true. I'm not a bully.' And he said, 'Well, prove it.' And it was just the most amazing bit of psychology, because I just thought, 'I'm going to.'

I had been at the school for two or three weeks, and they could see that I was behind with my basics. And he said, 'We're going to get you someone who can help you.' And I met this woman, Mrs Bowen. I went to her house, which was a short walk from the school, and she said, 'Right. They've told me you need to get your English up to speed.' She was just the most amazing teacher. She threw *The Guardian* at me, and said, 'Well, read that.' I said, 'But, I can't read.' She said, 'You can't read?' I said, 'No, I can't read.' She said, 'Look, you can't be 15 and not be able to read. Just look at the pictures and see if any of the words help you to understand. What do they tell you?' And basically, in the space of an hour, she convinced me I wasn't thick and that I could read. And then she taught me phonics. That's why I'm such an advocate. You need a mix of teaching around reading, but I think phonics is a good starting point.

And the rest is history. I was elected Head Boy and got 10 GCEs as they were in those days. I didn't do A-levels because I got there too late, but I got enough qualifications to get into college. But, you know, it was Jim Rudden saying, 'Prove you're not a bully.' And then Mrs Bowen saying, 'I'll rote teach you how to get good grades in your exams.' She taught me about exam technique. I'm not a great speller now, but she taught me 20 *magic words* to use, like 'salient' and 'reciprocity'. And I rote learned how to spell them and what they meant. And she said, 'Whatever questions come up in your English essays, you've got to find a way of getting those words in.' And the fact that I passed English language is unbelievable! This is why I'm so obsessed with getting kids to be able to read and write properly. In 20 years, I've never failed to teach someone to read and write, and most recently, I've been teaching a builder who's been working at my house how to read.

So, anyway, that's why I'm such an advocate for English and maths. You can make it interesting for kids, particularly around applied learning. And particularly if you're saying to kids, 'If you can't read a wage packet, you're going to get ripped off.' We used to do weird things like teach kids maths while playing darts... but we'd say, 'You can only play darts if you can add up and subtract.' And then we'd say, 'Well, you can go go-karting, but you can't fill a form in. So, as we're going in six weeks, you've got six weeks to learn how to fill the form in.' I know it's very carrot-and-stick and some people point out it's not very ethical, but guess what? If kids get five GCSEs or they leave school with the ability to read and write, there's less chance they're going to go to prison. And I've got no *action research* to prove that. But with all my 40 years of experience of working with kids with challenging behaviour, I know if they can leave school being able to read and write, knowing how to be assertive rather than aggressive, understanding social skills and applied learning, then they've got a fighting chance.

The gift you bring to both this conversation and the wider discourse is your deep-rooted experience. Things like teasing young people into learning, how you want the students back into mainstream pretty damned quick by the end of KS3, and the idea that we're never going to teach you anything that you don't need to learn.

Towards the end of my time there we managed to employ a brilliant bloke to work with us. He came in and did two things. One, he introduced Philosophy for Children (P for C), and he challenged kids morally around their behaviours using the Philosophy for Children. And the other thing he did – and it's really sad to have to say this – was to introduce a first-aid triage course, which taught children what to do, God forbid, if one of their friends got stabbed and how to manage that situation, because the reality is that for many of the youngsters we worked with, that was going to happen. That was part of the core curriculum as an element of *preparation for life*.

And that's a hard-nosed take on the therapeutic curriculum. The reality is that they do need to know this. I think that's being completely unsentimental and realistic and preventative. There is a question I'd like to ask and it's this: 'Are there any children you felt you didn't reach in one way or another?'

What we did for some children was get them through school. What we didn't do for *all* of them was reignite that love of learning. Education's never wasted. It might take 20 years before you see the benefits, but if you can make a person feel positive about learning and life, they can be successful. That's why I say the curriculum has to be alternative and compensatory because sometimes it takes as long to sort troubled children out as it takes to create their troubles. So, if you pick up a 14-year-old, it might take another 14 years for them to get sorted. And so, the best you can do in the 18 months or two years that you've got them is get them to a base point where they can springboard off. In my experience, most of the youngsters who did well, did well from 18 onwards. They left school at 16, they mucked about for a bit, did lots of informal things. Although most of them left school and went to college, they dropped out by half-term because college didn't give them the love and the care that they needed to know it's safe here to fail. This is the big thing I think people forget: children won't learn if they don't feel safe. You must make a PRU and AP physically safe, but you must make it emotionally safe as well. So, these youngsters, they go off to college and they break down in six weeks because there's not enough support for them. But by the time they're 18 and they realise – and I don't mean this in a pejorative way – they can't get a *real* job as opposed to just cash in hand all the time, they then get back into training and working hard. The skill, then, is keeping in contact with them so that they still want to go back to college.

What's hard about that is all the relentless effort that you make for them at 14, 15, 16 often gets thrown back at you. You've got to trust that it's an investment in the bank for later.

My sister Julia had cerebral palsy and my mum's endlessly trying to talk to her to make her talk. It took 20 years before she could talk. But it was worth it – it's *always* worth it – because in the end she spoke. And this is at the heart of AP – seeing children for what they can become rather than how they're behaving. If you just look at the behaviour, you can understand, possibly, why they are there, because you know the experiences they've had, but if you can't look beyond that and give unconditional positive regard, you can't set them up to make the most of themselves. Whereas, if you say, 'It doesn't matter what you throw at me, I can withstand it,' they have a chance.

But boundaries are so important. I love children, but boundaries have got to be there. The adults have to be in charge in all schools, but particularly in the context of a potentially unsafe situation. You've got 20 young men, who are all six foot and they're all gang members and they're all wheeling and dealing, saying to you, 'I earn more in one night than you earn in a week.' You need strict boundaries. So, for some children, you sow the seed and it might take 10 years to germinate. Ironically, sometimes I still get kids from prison writing to me, and I say to them, 'Well, you didn't listen well enough in school, but you've just got to listen hard now. Do your time and then learn from this experience as well.' So, education is never wasted.

Another thing one of my colleagues did was put up a sign at the front of the door that said, 'Are you ready to take up your place as a learner?'

And he said, 'John, I want to do this – if they're not, I need to have a space that they can go to before they are ready.' It's brilliant. Because some kids come to school, they come every day because they know they're going to get fed, they're loved, but they're not emotionally available to become a learner. But by the time they've had half an hour of TLC, or you've changed their bandages on stab wounds or whatever, you then say, 'Now we do some maths.' So, I think that notion of being ready to take up your place as a learner is challenging the child at the start of the day.

The other big thing, and it took me years to understand this, is use of descriptive praise. Don't just tell kids their behaviour is or isn't okay; tell them what it is about their behaviour you like or dislike, so they understand. In the same way, if a kid gets a sum wrong, you say, 'I like the effort you made, I see you worked really hard on that. Let's try to unpick why you didn't get it right.'

So, if someone's behaving, you say, 'It's nice to see you sitting nicely,' or 'It's nice to see that you've really tried to do your tie up straight.' So, you're describing why you're praising them. And that is infectious. And it took me a long time to realise just how powerful that is, but it's a real golden nugget. That's not to say you don't tell kids off, but even when you tell them off, you describe what it is about their behaviour that means they're being told off.

And then the other thing is – and this is a real Catholic bit coming out – reparation, the great Bill Rogers line – the certainty of the consequence is more important than the severity. You get something wrong, you've got to put it right. And that's not punishment, that's a sanction. No, punishment doesn't work. We all know that sanctions work, but not punishment. And a lot of people need to learn the difference between the two, but reparation is a big part of that.

What would you say is the difference between a sanction and a punishment?

Punishment's arbitrary. You might come in one day without your tie on and I put you in detention. The next day you come in and I'll let you put your tie on, and I won't put you in detention. If the rule is you must wear a tie, there must be a set consequence for not wearing a tie, and that's a sanction. So, punishments are arbitrary, in my experience, and they're more about the individual. There's a consequence for appropriate behaviour, and there's a consequence for inappropriate behaviour. Not anything goes; there must be a consequence for appropriate behaviour and a consequence for inappropriate behaviour. Sanctions are a type of behavioural feedback.

I think sanctions are okay – I've got no problem with sanctions, but they're not punishments. And I think it's that arbitrary nature of punishments that makes them not work. Because kids don't know where they are. Whereas if you say, 'Every time you drop litter, you've got five minutes litter picking,' and it always happens, that is a sanction. And you don't need many rules. What you need is principles. In the secondary department of the school, we had three: be safe, show respect, follow instructions. Bang. Very simple. You need principles, and you incorporate the rules into the principles. The single most important thing to me was that kids were safe. This is a learning institution. It must be safe. And it was written on every wall, and you can do anything around that. You can get round any *rule* that you want, but principles are really effective. The curriculum has to work so that you can take the risks of learning that you need to do. I'm not having kids come into school thinking, 'Am I going to get stabbed in this lesson if we blow up?' Because things happen. We ensured the kids left their weapons outside. We would walk them to the bus stop and make sure they got on the buses. I'm not responsible for what happens when they get home, but I can make sure they get home safely.

What's coming through is much more emphasis on student voice and student responsibility. There's a lot of choice-making that you're offering these children.

In life, they're going to have to make those choices, aren't they? If they're going to have to learn these skills anyway, why not teach them early? You know, if you can teach someone who's aggressive to be assertive, well, why not do it at 14 and 15, rather than wait till they're 25 and they've been banged around in the penal system? I'd say to our heads, 'Look, this kid is going to be all right, but he needs a bit of TLC and just make sure, when he comes into school, you make him do 10 laps of the gym, because he needs to get the cortisol out of him.' And people would laugh at me, but it would work. The first thing we did every morning in KS3 was make the kids do some PE, because they'd been in a taxi for ages.

Before we finish, I'd just like to try to differentiate between mainstream SEND and AP. I think there are some overlaps...

Well, when you say that someone's behaviour is 'inappropriate', that word is a social construct and is bound up with the notion of normative categories and non-normative categories. So, my sister was in a normative category. She was a wheelchair user. She had cerebral palsy. You could quantify that. For someone to say to me that my behaviour in school was 'inappropriate' depended upon society's definition of 'normal' in that context. In other situations, like playing football at the weekend as a 14-year-old with 21-year-olds, that same behaviour would have been labelled 'appropriate'. In that footballing context I needed to be aggressive to survive. Of course, there was something wrong with the way I was behaving, but there was also something wrong about the context and the construct that says 'here's someone who can't behave'. Now in relation to SEND and AP, there were many children in my experience in AP who should have or could have benefited from having an EHC plan but weren't in the special school. And equally in the special school, there were some children who would have been better suited to being in the PRU. And if I'm being honest, informally, because we were a group with such a range of provision, we could facilitate having students on the roll of the PRU for whatever bit of their curriculum, but then they would come into the school for the lessons. And some kids in the school would go to the PRU for lessons. And guess what? Outside of school, they were the same kids and they mixed together.

And I will never forget when I interviewed a kid who was leaving us. He said to me, 'But next week, sir, when I leave school, I won't have any special needs anymore, will I?' And I said, 'Why is that?' He said, 'Well, because I've got a statement that says I have to come to New Rush Hall, but what happens to my special needs next week when I leave and I don't have to come here any longer?' And that comes back to that whole notion of the social construction of disability and why some kids end up in PRUs and why some kids don't.

I think building trust in AP is a big part of the work. For example, we used to take kids climbing. I'd take two great big strapping kids. I'd get roped up and I'd say, 'Right, I'm going to climb up that thing and I want you to hold the rope.' I felt confident enough to know that I wouldn't have fallen off. And the great thing was when you came down, the kids said, 'I've done it. I've just helped sir climb.' Now, trust is a two-way thing. Kids have got to trust you to learn. Learning is a risky business, particularly if you've got no self-esteem – you can't afford to get it wrong. That's why kids join you. Kids don't work if they're frightened of getting it wrong. So, if you take that away from them, they have to succeed, they will make progress, they will trust you. And I don't mean it in an egotistical way: 'Oh, you can trust me, I'm a safe teacher.' They think, 'I'll behave for him because he's going to make me learn to read better. And I'm going to behave because he makes me read better, and I'll be safe.'

Alternative provision, not inferior provision

A conversation with Gerry Robinson

Gerry Robinson is executive head of Haringey Learning Partnership.

John Tomsett (JT): Hi Gerry. Please could you talk to us about what you do?

Gerry Robinson (GR): Haringey Learning Partnership (HLP) is the alternative provision offer in Haringey and includes several different provisions: Commerce House, which is what many would call the 'PRU' (although we don't use this term with our young people or staff) for those who have been excluded, or are at risk of exclusion, from mainstream school, or those who are experiencing difficulties being in mainstream school, possibly because of emotionally-based school avoidance; a medical needs provision for young people who are unwell and need an alternative means of accessing education; and Simmons House, which is a psychiatric inpatient provision within a hospital setting. We also have quite extensive outreach services working with mainstream schools to support inclusion in mainstream.

JT: Tell us a bit about how the curriculum is designed at Commerce House.

GR: Of all of our provisions, the curriculum at Commerce House is the one most similar to a mainstream school curriculum. I was really clear, when I came into HLP three and a half years ago, that we needed to make sure that the expectations of our young people were raised quite significantly. I found a narrowing of the curriculum, coupled with really low expectations around what young people could achieve in alternative provision. There was no science on the curriculum, for example. If you were referred to Commerce House, you would not study science for a year and a half and then you'd be expected to go back into a mainstream school and be successful. Clearly, that was going to make things significantly more difficult for young people if they did reintegrate into mainstream because the gaps in their learning would have widened massively. But it also said to those young people that we didn't think they were capable of academic excellence, or that their provision should be limited because they wouldn't be able to cope with a full curriculum offer.

I think many young people come into alternative provision quite traumatised and having had a very negative experience of schooling. They've been sent a message that they're not good enough or that they don't fit in. What we needed to do, quite rapidly, was improve our young people's sense of worth, their confidence in themselves, their ability to see themselves as successful learners. If they come into alternative provision and they're met with a much narrower curriculum and low expectations, then we're just reinforcing those messages that they might have previously heard.

It's been really important to me to lift our expectations of young people; consequently, the curriculum offer at Commerce House is very similar to a mainstream school. In some cases, we have young people studying eight or nine GCSEs, just as they might in a mainstream setting. While we do have the option to build bespoke plans for our young people, if a young person is able to access that number of qualifications, then they should be able to do that. I always say to people, 'It's alternative provision, not inferior provision.'

JT: Is there anything else that's broader that's maybe compensatory or different and meets their additional needs?

GR: Absolutely, we also look to expand that beyond the mainstream curriculum. In fact, many of our young people get a *better* curriculum offer with us. We're very focused on enrichment opportunities as a means of re-engaging students with education and supporting their personal development. As a result, our young people have many more enrichment opportunities than they've had previously in mainstream schools. They're often the young people who haven't been on many school trips, who haven't been included in extracurricular opportunities because of behaviour and concerns around them taking part. So, we work with organisations like First Story, where our students complete a young writers' programme, which sees them working with a published author over 16 weeks and becoming published writers themselves by the end of the course. The publication of their work is marked by a book launch, a big celebration event to which we invite the young people's families and their previous schools to hear them share their work. We also work in partnership with Jamie's Farm, which is a brilliant organisation with a focus on nurture and relational approaches. We have a group of young people who attend a farm based in Waterloo every Friday and that's part of their curriculum offer. But we also have young people who don't do that regular Friday, but enjoy a week-long residential to Jamie's Farm in Monmouth, Wales. They come back so motivated and inspired, full of stories of that experience, because it's so different to their regular lives. Similarly, we work with an organisation called Haringey Play Association; the work we do with them is funded by the London Violence Reduction Unit, which enables a group of our young people to take part in construction every Friday. But it's not just about teaching construction skills; the project involves renovating and developing a local community playground, which supports students to give back to the community they are growing up in.

Many of these opportunities are about changing the perception of our young people – how other people outside of the organisation see them – but also changing the young people's perceptions of themselves. You can be a published author and have a book that's in the British Library. You can go and live on a farm in Wales for a week and be successful. You can contribute to a community playground and be recognised for the contribution you made. It does a lot for our young people's sense of self-worth and changes some of the ways our young people are seen by people external to them.

JT: I'm interested in how you manage the curriculum for children with medical needs.

GR: The young people with medical needs often have significant gaps in their learning, which is a common thread for young people coming into alternative provision. We try to work out where those gaps are and then work to help bridge them. The aim could be to return them to a mainstream setting and what we don't want to do is make it harder than it needs to be. A lot of our young people with medical needs have one-to-one tuition, particularly if there's a young person whose immune system is compromised – they can't learn in a group of other young people so they might be having tuition at home. We're not sending nine different subject teachers to their home; rather, it's thinking about the curriculum offer and how we deploy the specialist teaching and where we can make that happen.

To support pupils, we've created 'pop-up' science labs, so that some home-based, safe experiments can happen. We try to replicate, as far as is possible, the experience that they would have had in the mainstream classroom. And obviously, if they are with us for medical needs, they will be on dual-roll with their mainstream school. We work closely with their mainstream school to ensure we are following the curriculum the young people would have been following had they been in school. Keeping up that regular contact is so important for the young person, to prevent them feeling forgotten about or not invested in. It might not be the mainstream school delivering the curriculum, but I think it's important that they're aware that connection is still there. We ensure they have work they can then share with their school, so they get a sense of achievement from being able to say, 'I have something tangible in front of me that I can share with my school. I wasn't there, but I did do this.' That's been important for many of our young people with medical needs.

JT: Sir Simon Wessely, the Regius professor of psychiatry at King's, cites a study that looked at children who were really up against it, who had everything stacked against them. It was a longitudinal study over 40 years. Of that group of children in dreadfully challenging circumstances, the ones who were successful later in life were the ones who were good at something. Early success is important for children; it seems to me to be important for their self-worth. They've had their dignity destroyed time and time again, and they just want to be able to be proud of something. Does that resonate with you?

GR: It's important for our young people to have work they can be proud of, so we invest a lot of time into increasing their sense of self-worth. One example that springs to mind is that as part of our last Black History Month event our young people put on a photography exhibition linked to some beautiful paintings that they'd created. It was called *Saluting Our Sisters* and so they had photographed many of our black female staff in the school. They then asked them questions about their favourite places. They painted these settings, and they displayed their art in school. Seeing the pride in our young people as they took visitors around and showed them the work, whether it was a family member or the mayor of Haringey, was enormous. Even since then, we had one parent who came one day and then the next day brought her sister in – the young person's aunt – and asked, 'Is the artwork still up? Can I show it to her?' The parent was so overjoyed to see something so special that their daughter had done in school – they couldn't wait to show it off to other family members. If we can build on those successes, it can change everything for a young person.

Mary Myatt (MM): You can't make that, you know, that can't be manufactured. That comes from an authentic, deep space. So, you have a more robust, appropriate curriculum in place – the opposite of what I call a diminished diet. What are the students' attitudes like now, would you say, compared to four years ago, before the curriculum was ramped up and the wider provision put in place?

GR: It's important to listen to what the students are saying, and we do that a lot, but I think the improvement is evident in things like attendance rates. Now, we have attendance of about 92%. That's in line with mainstream schools and higher than many mainstream schools, post-COVID. When I started here, the attendance rate was just over 50%; in some terms, it would dip below 50%. And I think that tells me so much about how much the young people value coming to school, because they know that they are coming here to do something meaningful. Before, there was a sense of, 'Well, there's not really any point. We're not studying GCSEs and we're not going to be doing science or some of the subjects that we do in mainstream school so what's the point?' In past times, they just wouldn't come in, or if they did come in, there was a tendency to take the young people out of the classroom for a walk or to play table tennis or to go into the gym and play basketball, rather than to be in the lessons and learning. The young people have told me that it created a youth-club vibe and the value in being there was lost. The behaviour was incredibly challenging. But I think when you have well-planned, well-structured lessons, high expectations, wrap-around care and all of the enrichment, then you can reasonably quickly change the whole culture of the school.

JT: I wonder how the mainstream schools have responded to the work you're doing here?

GR: As a former mainstream headteacher in the borough, I had pre-existing relationships with local headteachers and good relationships with our schools. That's been helpful. So, when I've invited heads to come and see what the young people are doing, they've come. That's been important both for the staff and for the young people. Exclusion can be such a difficult thing – being told you're not wanted somewhere, facing judgement from those around you, losing your friendships, all you've known. And when it does happen, there are ways in which it can be done that can be much more supportive to a young person.

People talk about there being that rupture, but also the need for the repair. After a young person's come to us, even if they're not going back to that mainstream school, if the deputy head or the head of year comes to visit and talks to them about the work they're doing, it helps mend that relationship a bit. Otherwise, it can leave a young person traumatised and resentful, which isn't healthy for the school or for the young person. And then we have schools wanting to come back again and again to see how that young person is doing. And then, hopefully, we restore their sense of self-worth.

MM: You're talking about compassion, but tough compassion. They deserve a good, strong, demanding curriculum. But that light-touch, ongoing contact with the children is something that's going to be picked up by people who aren't specialists in this field. Neil Miller, the deputy CEO of the London South East Academies Trust, told us they track their young people for two years after they leave at the end of Year 11. It's about whether you can be bothered, and then if you can be bothered, you've got the capacity to do something about it because it's difficult, human-resource-intensive work, but crucial for these children's futures.

GR: Similarly, if a young person's moving from us back into a mainstream school, we continue that support. It will look different for each child – some require long-term outreach support, whereas others are ready to move forward and can do so independently quite quickly, so may just have a few visits and phone calls to check in. We try to work with mainstream schools and families to work out what each child needs and adapt accordingly.

JT: Tell us a little bit about your outreach work with mainstream schools, where you have got to build the capacity to support students who, in the past, may have been excluded and sent to AP.

GR: You read in the news about the numbers of young people coming into AP – PRUs with waiting lists because there are so many children being excluded from school or being moved into AP for other reasons. Post COVID, I think the landscape is different for young people; we're seeing significantly increased presentations around mental health, quite often more challenging behaviour, and so we've had to respond to that because mainstream schools need to support young people in ways that maybe they haven't had to before.

Outreach was quite a key part of developing our organisation. Back in September 2020, one of the first things we did was build our outreach teams. We have a primary outreach team and a secondary outreach team, and then we have a team that's focused solely on transition from Year 6 into Year 7. The team is reasonably big, but we could do with a team five times the size because the number of referrals for that support is growing relentlessly. Outreach involves some direct work with the children and young people, but it's much more about working with the adults around those children. We want to build sustainable practice, to build inclusive systems where any young person can be supported in mainstream, and signpost where else schools can get support. We offer training to schools, helping them develop individual learning plans for young people, meeting with teams of teachers around a child to share strategies. That work's been so important and it's had a huge impact in Haringey in reducing our permanent exclusion figures, bucking the trend at a time when we see permanent exclusions increasing nationally, and I think that's been down to the work to support young people to be successful in mainstream wherever possible.

MM: So, you've bucked the trend in terms of school attendance, and you've bucked the trend in terms of permanent exclusions as a local authority. That's extraordinary.

GR: Yeah. It's been a lot of hard graft from a lot of dedicated professionals!

MM: So, what do you think the next steps are in terms of developing your organisation to continue that impact?

GR: The biggest growth area for us, in terms of increased referrals, is around anxiety. And I think schools are having to rethink and develop what they're doing in this respect. I think we have to work in partnership with schools again, to work with them to develop strategies to keep young people in school. It's not always the best thing that the young person who feels anxious comes out of school and into alternative provision. There may be other things that we can do that keep them connected to their school and enable them to remain in mainstream and be successful. Obviously, we have to look at each child on an individual basis, but I think that's an area for us in terms of continuing to develop.

There is also developing our outreach work, focusing on how we prepare our young people for reintegrating into mainstream. We have very high rates of reintegration. Our headteachers in Haringey work in partnership with us to give young people opportunities to return. And we talk a lot about how we make sure that our young people are best equipped for that return. It's difficult to go back into a mainstream school – or to join a new mainstream school, with a new peer group, usually part way through the year – after you've already had a very negative experience of mainstream school. As much as we've worked to change it, people often hold the young person who is reintegrating to a higher standard than everybody else. We're doing a lot of work around how we make sure our young people are prepared. That's why we have such high expectations at Commerce House around things like school uniform and wearing school shoes. And all of those things can seem like quite trivial things, but all but one of the Haringey schools have a school uniform. So, if our young people are wearing their jeans and tracksuits and trainers, when they go back into a mainstream school the first thing they get into trouble for is that they're wearing trainers and not school shoes. That negative cycle begins immediately on return. We explain to the young people that that's why we're doing what we're doing. It's about helping to support you. They understand it. You know, it's not just some nonsense rule because we like to be in control; it's actually about helping you to be successful back in mainstream.

Similarly, when we teach an academically rigorous curriculum, it's to help our young people prepare for moving back into mainstream schools. We do a lot to find out which exam boards are being studied in which schools and which texts are being studied in English literature at GCSE, for instance, so we can make sure that those gaps are not growing while our kids are out of school. And all schools study different texts, but there are particular texts that are studied more frequently than others and we try to ensure our young people study those texts and keep up with their mainstream studies.

JT: Just to finish, what is the curriculum like for those children who spend time as inpatients in Simmons House?

GR: I think Simmons House is quite different in terms of our curriculum offer. It's important that we engage with our young people at Simmons House. And that means that their curriculum offer can look quite different and can be based upon what a young person might be particularly interested in. If you're at a point where a young person is a tier four patient in a psychiatric provision at 14 or 15 years of age, and there's a risk that they're thinking of ending their own life, then the most important thing we can do is find something that they can enjoy and be good at and see a purpose in and be passionate about. And it doesn't really matter what that is. So, we've had a young person who wanted to study Latin. We didn't have a Latin teacher, but we found some Latin texts and we worked it out together. And that young person was really focused on making sure that they could make progress in Latin. And that kept them well enough to be discharged from Simmons House eventually. And while that's not necessarily going to be the traditional English, maths and science curriculum, it's the most important thing that we can do because the challenges are different. It's about adapting the curriculum to where that young person is, meeting them where they're at, making sure again that they can see themselves as being successful, have pride in what they're doing and see a reason for being here. The latter is the most important thing. And that's why things like functional skills exams or unit awards can be really useful in Simmons House, because sometimes for young people it's that tangible 'I've achieved something and I've got a certificate that says I have this qualification' moment for a young person who felt like they were never going to achieve anything because they probably wouldn't be here.

It's definitely got to be more bespoke and the young people are taught in a different way in our classroom setting – each young person has their own station set up with their work and their plan of what they're going to be doing. And that could be completely different from the other 11 young people in the school setting. But that's okay. And you have to work hard to make that work, but it's definitely the right thing to do.

There's nothing particularly groundbreaking about what we do. I think it's just about seeing young people as young people who might have experienced different challenges, but they're still young people who deserve the very best. And when you invest that time, you show them that they're valued; it can change everything. If they can see themselves as learners, then that will carry them on to the next step, whether that's back into mainstream school, whether it's moving to a specialist setting, whether it's going into post-16 and on to college or an apprenticeship. Hopefully, when they move on from us, we've repaired some of that damage that might have been done earlier in their educational career.

Opening brand new doors

A conversation with Neil Miller

Neil Miller is the deputy CEO of the London South East Academies Trust.

Please could you tell us about your career history within alternative provision, Neil?

Prior to going into education, I was in the military. I was an army physical training instructor, so I went into secondary education in the South East as a PE teacher, but very quickly moved through the ranks. Because of my organisational and disciplinary skills, I was also able to work with some of the more challenging children. I was able to relate to them, probably because a lot of the blokes I worked with in the army had previously been as challenging as some of the children I encountered in school.

I was appointed deputy head at a secondary in Orpington in charge of behaviour and inclusion. Then I became the headteacher there. I've always, while in mainstream schools, gravitated towards the more challenging, disaffected young people. I was able to form good relationships with them and work with them effectively.

While I was at the school in Orpington, we created our own internal AP-style provision (when school budgets were a lot kinder). When I joined there, they were experiencing over 1000 days of exclusions per year. Attendance was extremely poor, and the number of permanent exclusions in the year before I joined was approximately 19. So, I really focused on working with the more challenging children and their families.

We created an internal AP unit for the most challenging young people. We reduced the number of exclusions to zero. Our attendance significantly improved. Our young people were leaving with qualifications and every young person who was leaving that particular provision was leaving with five GCSEs or equivalent, including English and maths. It was a real success. What I focused on while I was in mainstream was allocating the best teachers to the more challenging children. I would include myself in that, in terms of teaching them. I wouldn't expect anyone to be doing anything that I couldn't do myself. And I did cover, and goodness knows what else, for those groups. I felt it was important to lead from the front and set the standard of what we were expecting. By utilising the best teachers across the school, we managed to ensure that these young people were still engaged by the end of Year 11. We also focused on destinations for them. We worked closely with the local college and prioritised gaining them college places. Sadly, due to funding constraints, this provision model wasn't sustainable over time and the provision was significantly reduced in size and hence effectiveness.

Then the opportunity came to move to my present trust. They asked me to take over as the executive head of the two schools that were just starting with the trust, both failing schools. One was an all-through PRU from five to 16, and the other was an SEMH 11 to 16 boys' provision. When I joined the SEMH school, it had never been anything more than 'satisfactory' in Ofsted terms. We managed to move that to 'good with outstanding features' in 2019. The PRU was also failing in terms of previous performance. It was inspected in 2017 and achieved 'good'. Then it was inspected in February 2023, and achieved 'good with outstanding features'. Our trust has grown from those two schools to nine, with various other schools, including mainstream primary and other special schools due to be joining us very soon. We have a real mix within our trust of schools in four different boroughs. We have four SEMH schools – primary, secondary and all-through. We've got one secondary PMLD/

SLD special school, one large all-through ASD special school and one large mainstream primary.

Why did I join the trust? I'll be honest, the job and trust excited me. Firstly, because they were two failing schools and the sponsoring trust had the same vision and values as me. And secondly, it was the cohort of children and young people that were in them. They aligned with my moral compass. Those children weer being failed, and they had been systematically failed for many years. I felt I had the skill set, naively at first, to go in there and do wonderful things very, very quickly. There were only 32 children in the SEMH school compared to the school where I was headteacher, where there were 1500. Did I know that those 32 multiplied into about 500 in terms of their behaviours and everything else? Of course not, but I learned very rapidly!

What struck me very quickly was the work we needed to do to ensure that the quality of education and the curriculum were fit for purpose. What also became apparent very quickly was that the teaching staff across the schools needed to be developed. It wasn't the case that they couldn't provide what these children deserved; they just didn't have the tools to do it.

So, we brought in some expert teachers from my previous mainstream school who were previously working within our AP provision and doing a wonderful job. They provided training, support and expert teaching. We removed some of the staff quite rapidly. We also promoted some existing key staff to more senior positions who were highly skilled people to enhance the schools, and the impact was quite rapid.

In terms of the curriculum, across all our schools, but within AP especially, reading has been a real focus. At the end of the day, if the children can't read, then they're not going to be able to access any curriculum. And so we have put immense amounts of emphasis upon reading within our curriculum.

Recently we brought in a new director of school improvement. She was previously an Ofsted HMI and she led on reading nationally. So that's had a massive impact in terms of developing our pupils' love of reading. It's apparent in all our schools that reading is the absolute focus. We have a reading garden in the centre of our Bromley primary AP school, which is an amazing space where everyone is able to go to read on a daily basis.

Maths is another focus. Reading and maths, I would say, along with writing are the absolute focus within the APs, because they're the essential skills to allow those children to be literate and numerate moving forward into adulthood.

In terms of our secondary provision, every child in Year 11 has to leave with an English qualification, a maths qualification and a minimum of five GCSEs, or equivalent, graded 1 to 9. In terms of other subjects that they follow, they include GCSE qualifications in RE, food, design and technology, science, textiles and sport, etc. We insist upon a GCSE-based curriculum to give these children and young people the opportunities to be able to move on, while, at the same time, they can take vocational qualifications. We've just introduced construction provisions within our secondary APs to enable them to focus on vocational qualifications as well.

We're quite unique as a trust because we are sponsored by an FE/HE college and both of our APs are in the boroughs where our colleges are located. Consequently, we've got a great model for our young people to move from our APs into the colleges. Now that was why our trust was set up originally, because our visionary CEO, Dr Sam Parrett CBE, who was the principal at the college at the time, had identified that the children from those failing provisions were leaving the schools with zero qualifications. They were going on to college in September, and they were dropping out by October. Now every young person leaves with at least five GCSEs or equivalent, including English and maths. And then the vast majority move into our colleges.

It's not all about a vocational route through to post-16 vocational courses. Last year one of our young people left with 13 GCSEs or equivalents, including chemistry, physics and statistics. Our staff would stay behind and work with him on a personalised curriculum. He was a bright lad who made a stupid mistake; consequently, we wanted to do the very best for him. He went back into a sixth form mainstream school to study his A-levels of choice. We want to ensure that if young people come in with high prior attainment, we're able to move them forward. So, if they want to go back to sixth form mainstream, or to go on to study elsewhere, they can. The blueprint is there for our young people to aspire to go into FE.

In both our APs we have medical provisions. We've some bright pupils coming through who are obviously suffering with anxiety and mental health issues. And once again the qualifications they're gaining enable them to then move back into mainstream sixth form successfully.

One of the things that we did very early on, before the government created the legislation, was to create careers leaders within our APs to enable genuinely joined-up working with our partner organisations. They work closely with all the schools, the sixth forms, the FE colleges, etc., and, as a consequence, we have zero NEETs. And we've had zero NEETs for many years now across the trust, because we've got that absolute 'joined-upness' underpinning post-16 transition. Now sometimes they 'fall out', but we track them for two years and we 'push them back in'. If they do drop out of what they're doing, we have created positive relationships with the families to enable the families or the young person to contact us and say, 'Look, this course is not for me. Help me, please. I need to go/be going elsewhere.'

We also get young people onto apprenticeships and training through our work with the college, which is part of our group; it's a real strength of our organisation that we have that all-through approach.

We also created a 14 to 16 alternative provision within our college, run by our trust AP staff. Secondary headteachers in that borough identified that the AP provision that we were providing back in 2019 needed more variation to support a wider group of pupils. It was a proposal that we took to the headteachers and to the local authority and they all agreed to fund it. Now, young people from Year 10 go to college two days a week where they focus on vocational qualifications, either multi-skills, motor vehicle or hair and beauty, and then they do the other three days in school. They then move on to college post-16, straight on to Level 2 motor vehicle, or multi-skills or hair and beauty, which is a year in advance of their counterparts that leave school at 16 and move into college following predominantly Level 1 qualifications in those areas.

We've looked at how we can ensure engagement, because what's very clear is that these young people have been failed many times. They feel like absolute failures when they come to us. And I believe one of our real strengths – and this has been highlighted in every Ofsted inspection in the past few years – is personal development. We see personal development as the golden thread that runs through the whole curriculum. From children as young as five, right the way through to 16 and beyond, we focus on developing life skills and providing them with the skills to be able to move on to the next stage of their education or training. That has a massive impact in terms of engaging them and giving them the skills they need not only within school, but also the soft skills to be able to cope outside school.

A lot of our children come from quite dysfunctional families, from challenging backgrounds, and they live in challenging locations and mix with risky peer groups. We really focus on safeguarding because, as far as I'm concerned, if the children are not safe and the staff are not safe, then no one's going to learn, because the staff are not going to be able to deliver safely, and the children are not going to be able to learn because they feel scared the whole time.

So, as well as an academic education, we're trying to provide them with a holistic education, which gives them the skills to be able to make, hopefully, the right choices. And although we only see them 20% of their lives, and they're outside in the big scary world for the other 80% of their lives, we hope that we're providing them with essential skills that they can take with them.

I am a firm believer that developing relationships is the most important aspect. And I think it's 70% of the job. If you get that right, then actually, the rest comes quite easily. If you can't form relationships with these children and young people, then, while you might be the best teacher in the world, you're not going to be able to work with them.

When talking about relationships, I think class sizes are important. These children and young people have been failed in class sizes of 30 plus, with one teacher. A lot of it is to do with SEN and undiagnosed needs. We carried out baseline testing of one particular girl last year who came to us in Year 9, and she had a reading age of five years old. And I just despair. What has happened? That child has been let down so badly. That's why the absolute focus is on reading. And within a year she'd made huge progress, and her reading age had moved to 10 plus. It wasn't the case that she couldn't do it; it was a case that she hadn't been given the skills and the attention and the focus to enable her to do so. Our class sizes average from eight in primary AP to about 10 in secondary AP. We have a teacher in all classes and, where necessary (and where funding allows), we allocate teaching assistants. Our HLTAs do a significant number of interventions outside of the timetabled lessons to ensure that the core areas of reading, writing and maths can be caught up where the gaps have been identified through the baseline testing when the young people first arrive.

It seems to me that you can't force those relationships with the disaffected pupils. Can you learn how to get on with these children? Or is it something you either have as an adult, or you haven't?

I think it takes a particular skill set to be able to work in the AP sector. As I said, I worked in a mainstream school, where we had about 150 staff. Out of the 150 staff, although I would say 95% of them were brilliant, and they were really good teachers and support staff, etc., 140 of them just wouldn't have been able to cope with the stresses and strains that are present in AP and special schools. And that's not a criticism of them. It's just the fact that I do believe this job requires a particular skill set, and that you need a high level of resilience yourself and loads of compassion and empathy. But at the same time you need to be absolutely consistent with these young people, because that's something that they lack so much in their normal lives. They value having that consistency and having those boundaries that they have to work to because they haven't got it elsewhere, and they feel safe as a consequence.

You need the patience of a saint at times, but resilience is the key. They're going to come at you and test whether you are there for the right reasons. They've been let down so many times in their lives. Are you just going to be another person that lets them down? Are you going to be another person who's not going to be there when it matters? And I'll never forget it... this was when I first went to the SEMH school, because I took over the SEMH school at the same time as being the executive head for the AP. This school had been a failing school for 20 years, and they had had 10 headteachers the year before I joined. At Christmas time, as the pupils were leaving at the end of my first autumn term, one of the most challenging lads – but actually one of those lads who had real character (although, at times, when he was christening you with a number of different names, it wasn't so pleasant) – came up to me and said, 'Are you coming back in January?' A bit of a lump formed in my throat as he seemed quite emotional when he asked. And I replied, 'Of course, why wouldn't I?' I just saw this little half smile – he never smiled – and he just walked off home. That was quite telling. And that, for me, is the reason why I do the job, and why our staff do the job. I go into those different provisions on a day-to-day basis, and I'm humbled by what I see, in terms of the way the staff work with those pupils, the way they talk to them, the way they relate to them.

I don't think everyone can do it. When I moved to the SEMH and AP schools and about 15 to 20 staff followed me, it wasn't a criticism of the 140 staff I didn't ask. It was just that I thought they didn't have the skill set that was necessary to work with this group of children and young people. The stresses are very different in mainstream. It's all about progress and working in a class of 30 plus. And then primary school teachers having to be multifaceted and multiskilled to do the amazing job that they do. The pressures are enormous in mainstream, but they are different from the huge pressures in AP.

When you've got children coming in to school from hugely dysfunctional situations, it's like a tinder box at times. You don't know what's happened the night before. Some of those pupils haven't even been home. They've been walking the streets or doing whatever they've been doing the night before, and they're coming back into school. When you look at the levels of child protection, the levels of youth justice involvement of these pupils on a day-to-day basis, our staff do an incredible job. Our staff have absolute compassion for these children, but at the same time we are really quite robust with our systems, because if you give them an inch they'll take a mile. It's about boundaries.

Can you learn it? I don't think you can. I think you've either got the empathy that enables you to relate to these children, or you haven't.

So, thinking about your background, how have the military and sport helped shape your approach to curriculum?

Having served with some of the guys that I served with in the military, what struck me was that some of these lads couldn't read and write and when we went away – we didn't have mobile phones in those days, it was more like carrier pigeons – we used to get the blue letters from people back home, and the lads couldn't read them. So, I used to sit there and read the letters for them and then I used to write letters back. They were amazing people, but they were limited because of being illiterate and innumerate, and a lot of them didn't have functional families. The army was their family. The army created a safe place for them. That's ironic considering they were soldiers. But it did provide that safety net; it provided a family that they, probably, had never had. I came from a loving background – my mum and dad were very loving and supportive – but that was the career that I wanted. Until I went into the military, I was probably quite sheltered and then seeing the range of the lads that I served with created in me some empathy for them. That was the first moment when I knew I wanted to make a difference. I wanted to help them. As a consequence, when I came out of the army, I decided to become a teacher. I wanted to make sure every child and young person could read and write, and add up, take away and do the very basics. Those guys were amazing soldiers. They had really tight boundaries. There was absolute consistency there, and they thrived in that environment.

I think many people would probably call me really strict (and everything else at times), but actually, I think, I demonstrate respect. If you give respect, you gain respect; it's a real lesson that I learned in the army in bucket loads. I think that this definitely provided me with an advantage when I moved into teaching.

My sport was boxing. Again, it was a very disciplined, focused environment. The level of self-discipline you had to have to do well in that sport was incredible. Absolute focus. I think that helped me in terms of my levels of resilience when I went into the world of AP from mainstream, and took over a school that had had 10 headteachers the previous year, when they had all just walked out as they couldn't see how to make a difference. I needed discipline, respect, resilience, focus and to be totally driven to get through that, but it was absolutely worth it. Because at the centre of every decision was the pupils and making sure they get the very best.

What's the most left-field, innovative course or provision you've put on in AP?

We put on the Institute for Fiscal Studies (IFS) Level 2 Certificate in Financial Education. I wouldn't say it's particularly left field. But it's not your norm. We also put on a Chartered Management Institute (CMI) Level 2 in Management and Leadership. We provide courses that are going to give these young people skills for life.

So, the IFS qualification fills gaps in their education for life. When you come from a dysfunctional family, you're not going to be told about how to open a bank account, what interest rates mean, what credit cards do and things like that. Putting on a qualification such as the CMI course is more than a leadership course; it instils young people with self-confidence and the self-esteem so that they are able to actually stand up in front of their peers and deliver a session with PowerPoint slides and their own notes and, for many of them, they are in control for the first time.

We start the functional skills qualifications in numeracy, English and IT at Level 1, and then move on to Level 2. If they go to college, then they don't have to resit their English if they've got a Level 2 qualification. That's a massive positive for retention, because they can then just focus on that specialist vocational area, and their levels of engagement grow.

It just struck me then that we need a little bit more imagination when designing the curriculum for young people for whom alternative provision might be appropriate.

What we offer, Mary, has to be right for each individual child. And you know, a mainstream school of 1500 secondary school children, or 400 to 500 in a primary, isn't a fit for every single child. Without imaginative flexibility around what is on offer, they often fall out of education, or they're thrown out of education, as a consequence.

An AP unit is in between mainstream and the special school. And it can be really powerful and support those children, in a class of eight to 10, where their needs are being met. They're able to achieve. And isn't that the right thing we should be doing for these children? These young people with such awful back stories will struggle to cope in a class of 30 or 32. When they've got a reading age of five and they're studying at GCSE level, they're going to kick off.

And when I look at some of the horrific back stories to some of the pupils in our settings – they're carrying *that* amount of baggage in their personal lives. AP schools are often seen as the last-chance saloon. But actually, I think for some children, it's just the next chapter of their lives. We're opening brand new doors for them to enable them to move forward in their lives. They're not being written off. They're being given that really great opportunity to develop and grow as a consequence of all the amazing work that goes on in our trust.

We're here to educate you

A conversation with Amy Smith

Amy Smith is the director of education at the Surrey-based Inclusive Education Trust and the vice president of PRUsAP.

I oversee the running of all three AP academies in our trust. Two of those are 5-16 through schools and the third is a 5-11 school. We also run our alternative college, which is both online and face-to-face, for young people who are unable to access education, including many young people with anxiety or who are awaiting specialist provision, and those who don't quite fit anywhere in particular, but still need to be educated. The alternative college aims to re-engage pupils, focusing on maths and English, and building pupils' confidence and self-esteem. And finally, we run a lot of outreach work to support mainstream schools with managing young people who are exhibiting challenging behaviour.

Could you tell us about the challenges your young people are facing?

There are a lot of young people who are deemed to be, in inverted commas, 'badly behaved', but that's because they've got undiagnosed learning needs, so they're like square pegs in round holes in mainstream schools, and their needs haven't been identified. We've got a lot of young people who have experienced significant trauma and continue to suffer from its effects. We have young people who have significant mental health issues. Young people filter through to AP when they're in crisis, and then it's our job to figure out what's going on for each individual young person, shape appropriate provision for them and then move them to their next step, which is hopefully going to be successful for them educationally.

What are your principles underpinning curriculum design?

The main thing is that, while we're AP, we're still schools. That's the first thing we say to our young people: 'We're still a school, we're here to educate you, we just do it in a different way.' We try to give them a curriculum as broad as the curriculum they would get in a mainstream school. We are determined to avoid further disadvantaging these already disadvantaged young people by offering them a diminished, narrow curriculum. So, our staff are really flexible, in that they don't just deliver one subject. They might be a specialist in one subject, but they also have knowledge and skills in other areas. We deliver as broad a curriculum as we can possibly manage with the resources that we've got.

We don't have the facilities that mainstream schools have in terms of, for example, PE and science facilities, but we still do offer those subjects. We just do it differently. We have to be flexible and meet the needs of the young people. Some of our young people will do eight GCSEs, some of them will only do four equivalents, because it depends on the gaps in their learning, and their confidence.

We talk a lot about getting them ready to learn. So, there's a two-part curriculum. There's your academic curriculum, and then there's the pastoral curriculum where we're working with them on figuring out what's going on for them, and what's gone wrong for them. A lot of them arrive very angry about the education system. They feel that they haven't done anything wrong. They're the young people who are constantly being removed from lessons or being suspended or they're not attending school. So, we'll look at a curriculum that helps them to figure out who they are, how they learn and how to build their confidence so that they can learn. That's when we start to look at English, maths and any other subjects that they will need to get to their next destination, particularly if they're in KS4, so that they can go to college or on to an apprenticeship. They need to have qualifications to progress.

We review our curriculum every year – and sometimes even halfway through the year – because our cohorts are ever-changing, and what might work with one group might not work with another group. Our aim with KS3 is to move them on. We're not a forever school for those young people. So we're flexible in what we do. And we also listen to student voice. Sometimes we have young people who have been permanently excluded halfway through a GCSE course and it's one that we're not offering. So, we try to find a way for them to continue that qualification. As much as we've got a structure, the young people may all follow quite different courses within that structure to help them become the best versions of themselves that they can be. We want them to carry on with education and break the perpetual negative cycle that education has been for them.

All of our young people will sit GCSEs in English and maths and some other subjects, depending on what subjects we're doing in that particular cohort. We also offer Level 2 BTECs. But English and maths tend to be the subjects that our young people find really tricky, and they have a fear of failure. In maths, for example, when you track back, they've missed those foundations – the times tables, the number bonds. What they've done in a mainstream school is cover up that they don't understand – they've exhibited challenging behaviour because they know that that's going to get them out of what's a really difficult embarrassing situation for them.

Will they admit to setting a bomb off in maths because they knew they couldn't do it?

Initially they won't, but we will ask them, 'Why do you hate maths? Let's try to unpick it. Is it because when everyone else was learning times tables at school, you weren't there or you missed it or you were removed?' They don't fully understand how those foundations of maths are so important in helping them understand maths going forward. And so we have those really frank conversations. Almost without exception, they will own up because when you're in a one-to-one conversation with them, they feel that they can be honest with you. They know you're there trying to help them.

So, we help them build those basic skills. In the classroom, everyone starts off doing functional skills. Some will do Entry Level and some will do Level 1. Then they achieve that qualification because we don't put them in a qualification that we know will be too difficult for them. So, they achieve success. And then they start to do more. Then they'll do their Level 2, and then they'll sit GCSEs. When they reach the point of sitting the GCSEs, they believe that they can be successful. They've got confidence and they know they're going to find some of it hard but that's okay, they're going to give it their best shot. We take exactly the same approach in English and all of our other subjects. I call it a stepped approach to build their confidence. Because a certificate for the young people in AP means so much; they're not the kids that get certificates. And so actually to have something that they can take home and be proud of is transformational in terms of how they view themselves and learning.

You have reminded me of a line from Virgil: 'Success nourishes them: they can because they think they can.'

Yes, absolutely. We've had young people come in who have been brilliant at maths. We've put them in for early entry and then we get them to help the others in the class. In AP, encouraging kids to learn depends upon *relationships*, and not just working relationships with the staff but relationships with each other, so that they feel safe. When they arrive we explain that, 'Everyone's here for a reason and everyone has their story as to why they're here. They might not choose to tell their story but you all have a story and actually you might not choose to be here, and if we had our way, we wouldn't want you to be here, but you are here so let's make the best of it and let's do everything we can to get you where you want to be.'

Tell us more about the pastoral curriculum and what that does in terms of fostering those learning relationships.

In our secondary provision we have as many mentors as we do teachers. We don't have TAs, but our mentors are our 'bridge' to help build the initial relationship with the teacher. I'm a drama teacher by trade. When I first started working in PRUs and APs it was like walking into another world. They're all kids with no confidence at all, and there I am trying to teach them to be on stage and stand out. I learned very quickly that I had to build relationships with them. And if there was someone who they identified with more than me, like one of the mentors or the support staff, they would be that 'bridge'. No matter how cool and hip and happening I was, I was still a teacher and they still defined me as a teacher, and, in their minds, any teacher is part of the system that has got them to the place where they don't want to be. Our mentors have got lots of life experience that our young people can relate to; that doesn't mean the teachers don't, just that the mentors in particular do. Having that other person in the room with me, initially, really helped me to do what I needed to do with them. And I learned a lot about getting young people in a place where they're ready to learn. When we've got new teachers, I explain it's about helping our young people to figure out who they are and what they want. It's about them acknowledging the challenges that they've had and taking responsibility and being honest and having some ambition for the future. When they arrive in the morning, our mentors listen to what's happened last night; they allow the young people to offload how they feel and then get into a place to learn. We say, 'Don't let your past determine your future.' That's one of the mantras that the staff repeat to the young people. Bad stuff's happened, but you are in charge of your destiny. It's not the same for every young person. It's different for each one. It's bespoke.

A lot of the young people don't know what they want to do in the future. We have the responsibility for teaching them about the world in which they live outside of their very narrow experience. So, we do lots of trips, we go to the theatre, we go to museums. We have enrichment as a central part of our curriculum. Every half-term we run a day when the young people have to step outside of their comfort zone. They'll do things like kayaking, climbing or horse riding – things that are quite terrifying. But the staff will do it with them. We raise money for charity through a Christmas fair. They create products to sell and compete against all of our schools within the trust to raise the most money. We have another term where they give back to the community. They run the Senior Citizens Luncheon Club or they go to a special school – they've built a forest school in one of our local special schools. They might go to one of our other schools as part of Project Help Out. Everybody gets involved. And all of that's as important as our formal academic curriculum.

Your transition from drama teacher to the position you're in now has all been about your own learning.

Absolutely. We're learning every day. We're human beings and we will make mistakes just like the young people have made mistakes. I always say that bad stuff happens to make you better at the good stuff. But that's part of our ethos and I think you find that in a lot of APs and PRUs. That's why we have staff who were in PRUs and APs themselves many years ago, because they want to help people by using what they've learned themselves.

I just wondered if there was a sense of why mainstream schools have not been able to find the right tempo for these young people?

I worked in mainstream schools before working in AP. I think secondary schools are so big. You've got 30 children in a class and I think we're having to do more with less now. SENDCOs in schools are so stretched. I think they see the behaviour before they see anything else. We do a lot of training with the mainstream schools we work with, in terms of identifying what the student's behaviour is saying to the adult. Behaviour is a form of communication. I know there are some people who would disagree, but in my experience, it's absolutely true. I think teachers are just seeing the behaviour and their main priority is the majority who are doing the right thing. It's not a criticism, it's to do with the system. If you've got 30 in a class and one person is incredibly disruptive, the teacher – because of the pressures that they're under – is just seeing the behaviour. So, we do a lot of intervention work with our mainstream schools. We say, 'When you're starting to feel that something's not going right, when that young person's starting to get quite a lot of detentions or you're starting to suspend them, call us in and we will work with you.' We've had huge success in reducing permanent exclusions because we're identifying challenging young people with our mainstream colleagues; those colleagues learn the distress signs and are then able to identify other young people who might be vulnerable. That partnership is having huge success. It doesn't mean the young people need to leave their mainstream school; they just need a different approach, or their sensory issues addressed, or they just learn differently.

So, in your context, how do you make the curriculum well sequenced when you've got many of the young people for just a short period of time?

The ones who tend to be short-stay are KS3 and primary pupils. For these pupils, the curriculum is based on 12-week programmes. It will be project-based and the academic subjects are woven into the projects. We are cajoling the young people into learning, because as soon as we say we're going to do maths now, it becomes an issue and behaviour deteriorates. It's difficult to sequence the curriculum when they're short-stay pupils, but if you know what you want them to achieve within a 12-week period, it works. You have to work in chunks, and 12 weeks is the appropriate time for them to be with us, to develop the skills that they need to be successful in another school or specialist provision or whatever is the most appropriate setting for them once they move on from us.

We focus on the subject-specific building blocks at KS4. With the KS4 short-stay students we focus on filling the gaps in maths and English primarily. We have a system that identifies what they should have learned at the end of KS2 or KS3 and assess them against that. We do CATs testing as well to give us an indication of their general cognitive capabilities. But you can't do everything. So, it's the maths, English and getting them in a place to learn and enjoy being in a classroom.

To what extent is the demarcation between SEND and AP a false one?

I don't think it is. I think we are a separate entity. We are the middleman between mainstream and SEND. We're the ones who they come to in absolute crisis. We're the ones who have to challenge their behaviour, help them regulate their behaviour, and try to unpick what's gone wrong.

It's like a whirlwind when they arrive and they're angry and they're frustrated and they hate everything. They're really confused and our job is to level them out so that when we hand them over to specialist provisions, they can then start to do the long work towards adulthood. We work collaboratively, but we are separate. Special school staff are specialists. So, if you're a young person with ASD and you're going to an ASD school, the staff know so much more than we do about ASD. We have enough knowledge of ASD in the short term, whereas colleagues in special schools know about it for the long game.

We work with mainstream more and more. Gone are the days where we were the dumping ground for mainstream schools. We work to support them, we learn from them and we network with our mainstream colleagues from a curriculum perspective. You can be quite isolated if you're a maths teacher – you might be the only one in an AP setting. We want to keep up to date with everything that's going on, and the same kind of networking happens with our SEND colleagues. We are unique in our own right, and I think that's been much more widely recognised now. But it's all a partnership; none of us can do our jobs without the others.

There are always going to be children who don't fit in mainstream schools who need something different. But the work we should be doing is supporting mainstream schools to keep the vast majority of children currently referred to AP in their schools. And that's not just us, that's in partnership with the local authority, CAMHS, etc. I'm hoping that with the situation we find ourselves in – with permanent exclusions skyrocketing – someone's going to take a look and say, 'Okay, how can we do this differently?'

I'm interested in your trust. What makes your organisation stand out? What is it that you'd love to tell us that you think is pretty special?

I think we're really innovative and we're not scared to take risks.

Please give us a concrete example of what you mean by that.

We're not scared to do anything. When I first started working in PRUs, as a drama teacher I wanted to do a show, and I wanted kids from each of the schools in the trust to be in the show. The SLT said it would not work. And I was like, 'Well, why not? They're all young people, they just live in different places.' Of course, I was aware of the potential issues. But we perpetuate the negative stereotype of the PRU student if we don't show them that they can put on a show. So, we had the most amazing time because they all realised that they were the same, despite coming from different neighbourhoods. Yes, they lived in different parts of the city, they were in different gangs, but deep down, they were all young people, who'd all faced challenges, who all loved drama.

The CEO of our trust is a PE teacher and he's not scared to let me take them to the theatre. We have worked with the BRIT School for a number of years. The pupils do a project with the BRIT School students. And, you know, it's hard work because a lot of them don't want to go, they're terrified. But by the end of it, it's the best thing ever.

And we do residentials too. We're not scared to do something different. If it's right for the young people, then we'll give it a go. And if it goes wrong, we hold our hands up and say, 'Well, that didn't work very well, did it?' Because that's life and you learn from it and you do it differently and you move on. And that's what the kids who we work with need to learn. Things go wrong, but you can recover from it. And failure can be one of the best learning experiences ever.

Locality-wide commitment to high provision for pupils in AP

A conversation with Susie Weaver

Susie Weaver is the education director at Cabot Learning Federation.

Can you tell us how you got into the world of alternative provision?

I would describe myself as having been a SENDCO forever since I became one nearly 20 years ago in my second year of teaching. I started teaching in primary, and I now work with pupils aged from three to 19 as education director for the Cabot Learning Federation. I have been with the trust for about a decade. As part of this role I have the opportunity to work across a number of local authorities.

We have alternative provision within the trust, and I also have the opportunity to work within and beyond the trust across the sector. I chair the high needs working group in one of the local authorities and I'm also part of the current DfE alternative provision implementation steering group as we move from the Green Paper to the White Paper and into practice. I am interested in meeting the needs of all children with the view into AP from my role as education director.

We have several AP settings across the five clusters within the trust. The alternative provisions started more than 10 years ago in The Nest, one of our primary schools in East Central Bristol. We wanted to focus on supporting children with a range of needs in primary. We recognised that we would have to work differently in order to genuinely meet Maslow's needs for our pupils who need additional support.

We worked with leaders, teachers, children and their families to establish a formal AP setting across the age range with Engage as part of our first secondary alternative provision and then The Nest for primary-aged children. Responding to the need, the trust's provision has grown over the last decade. For example, we have a setting called Snowdon Village, one of the largest multi-site APs in the UK. This was established to support children whose needs were not being met through mainstream provision. More recently, we have worked with a number of other AP settings that have now become part of the trust.

We also have an outreach model where our experts in primary AP work closely with the primary schools. This has been a recent development, particularly post pandemic, to recognise that there is a need to enhance and augment our AP provision from three to 19 within the mainstream and into AP, and then, into special schools as well.

The Nest started with a small number of children on roll, originally for pupils in KS2, and subsequently provision for KS1. We've not provided AP provision for Early Years, but we have provided plenty of outreach for our Early-Years-aged children within the trust, as well as across Bristol.

We made sure that we recruited strong teachers and experts in alternative provision. Schools supported The Nest financially, regardless of whether they needed places for their pupils at the time or not, and I think that's one of the underpinning principles that has really helped us over time, because it wasn't about buying a place for a particular child at a moment of crisis. This approach was designed to counter the reactive, short-term responses that knock up against wanting to really develop deep and well-informed provision for children in alternative provision over time.

Because we had a commitment from all leaders in the schools in our trust to contribute and fund the provision, we were able to establish appropriate provision for children across the age range.

The partnership with the local authority has also been important. For example, if there's a child whose needs are not being met in their school, we would initially support them with some outreach, where experts from the alternative provision work with the teaching team and leadership team of the school where a child is on roll.

They would do some assessments and diagnoses, and they would visit the child in the setting. If appropriate, they would connect with the family and talk with the teaching team and with the leadership team. We have worked hard on processes, but most importantly, this is a relational thing. This is about establishing, 'Where is that child and what do they need? What would really help? Do they need the alternative provision approach, or is there something else?' And if it's something else, 'How can we work together? How can we still use the expertise through a partnership approach?'

We have also worked hard over time to be clear whether this is about a child who has special needs that might not be met in an alternative provision, because the design in AP focuses on a short-term placement to support a child to reintegrate back into mainstream. Both The Nest and Engage are built upon that principle. It means that if there is a child for whom it does not look as though that's an appropriate pathway, then we would continue to support them, but we would be quite careful not to place them in our alternative provision. This is because there is a risk that they might get stuck there and then may not access the specialist provision that they need, and it might also not be possible for them to return to their mainstream school.

We take great care with assessment, which is holistic and underpinned by a relational approach. If everyone who is part of the assessment conversation decides that there is a good fit, it would be followed by a careful process through starter days, becoming familiar with the new setting through careful integration. We are intentional about this process. For instance, pupils wear the uniform from their home school because we are working for reintegration after a successful placement. We want to maintain that connection with the school.

It means that the children in The Nest and Engage are all in different uniform. We make sure that pupils are clear about their own school and their team in The Nest and Engage. When they are ready to return to their home school, we make sure that it is a slow and gradual reintegration, and that it includes as much success building as possible so that the transitions are as positive and successful as possible.

Can you tell us about what pupils are taught and how you manage that?

Over time we have explored and wrestled with the curriculum. Is it our goal in these settings to make sure that children are ready and able to engage with learning when they return to their home school? Or is it about making sure that they are supported in smaller groups with people who understand their primary needs in a deeper way, and that those people also make sure that the children keep pace with the curriculum?

We have realised over time that, of course, it's a combination of all those things. There is a clear focus on supporting young people with whatever was causing them to not be able to engage in their mainstream lessons. Some support might relate to dispositions to learning, some to managing and self-regulating, where we use Thrive, a trauma-informed approach to improving the mental health and wellbeing of children and young people. When we are assessing children with social, emotional and mental health needs, we are doing this to work out where the gaps might be. We think about early experiences that some children might have missed out on, and therefore, what opportunities we need to plan for them in their learning to meet their developmental stages. We have placed emphasis on developing communication skills across all settings. It's also worth noting, in terms of Maslow's hierarchy of needs, that our alternative provisions have strong links with food banks and breakfast providers. We recognise that we have to place the Maslow stuff first, so we have breakfast and family dining, for example.

Sometimes we focus on dispositions in learning. And sometimes it's about the early experiences that might be missing. This can crop up when pupils encounter more challenging material either in the curriculum or in life, and so we try to help pupils to learn at that stage through the processes and experiences that they might have missed out on. So, we do have the sand tray out, and we have lots of the things that you might typically expect to see in an Early Years provision. We find there are children across the age range to engage in these. Similarly, in secondary, we do have children in arm bands learning to swim because they might have missed that part of their education. And we also have a really broad curriculum underpinned by English and maths and a strong focus on PSHE.

And there is a magic about the teaching team within the alternative provisions having strong relational approaches with the teaching teams of a pupil's home school. We support our pupils to understand the broad concepts appropriate for their chronological age range as well as their developmental age. We need to work to make sure that by the time they finish their placement at The Nest, Engage or one of our other settings, they are able to reintegrate into their curriculum in their year group in their home school with everything that sits behind that in their backpack.

Beyond the curriculum, do you offer any other opportunities?

One of the things we've been able to do as a result of being a group of schools working together is that we can offer a whole suite of qualifications and engagement in lessons that wouldn't be possible in a standalone AP setting. Within the secondary age range, and particularly through the Snowdon Village model, the design of that curriculum is based on the idea of forest school provision, but rather than a focus on outdoor learning, the curriculum design is based on using the city as the location and environment for a host of learning experiences, with the idea of a city within a school.

It is about providing pupils with rich and meaningful learning experiences that are tangible and that also give them entitlement and opportunity. We can use the resources around us, and that is what good SEND provision and what good Early Years provision does in spades, anyway. And we were obviously trying to make sure that it was as equitable as possible. In one of our settings, the City School provision goes beyond the national curriculum to create a platform for the learning to seem meaningful.

In all our primaries, and particularly in the alternative provision, we are always focused on making sure that the learning has context – that it has meaning. And it's described in a way that develops agency for our young people. Our curriculum statement is built on developing a sense of agency, a sense of self and a sense of place. And then the development of key concepts, understanding and their knowledge. We deliberately wrote that curriculum statement in that order. What we're seeking is agency. What we're ultimately interested in is the children having a strong understanding of the concepts across the curriculum, but also to develop a sense of self, a sense of place and agency and creating that strong sense of belonging for all.

This is particularly important to develop in AP settings, because that sense of self, of place and of agency is one of the things that's potentially been eroded. As a result, we have tried to really lean into that.

We have schools in seaside towns and cities and across rural areas, and we serve five communities in the Southwest. We have held firm to the idea that pupils will have the national curriculum, content and concepts. And we also have the opportunities and the freedoms within AP that mean we can use the environment and the community in a way that might not be as straightforward in our mainstream settings. We have intentionally fostered very strong, deep and meaningful relationships with our communities where our AP settings are based.

This means we have positive connections with local businesses and communities so that they can provide a platform for the learning experiences. For example, if there is a music studio nearby, and we have a young person who's really interested in expressing his oral skills and focuses on oracy, we might look to develop this through music. That young person might have an individually crafted music session in a studio that gives them the opportunity to have a platform for their oracy work.

We look for those opportunities through the individual lens of what an individual child needs in their learning and as a result there is a myriad of provisions across the AP settings that use their community to provide that platform for purposeful engagement in real learning.

I'm wondering about the level of professional collaboration that needs to be in place in order to make this work.

There is considerable collaboration, and the schools in the trust engage with the full process. We make sure we work closely with leadership and teaching teams, together with our families and mainstream settings. We've created systems such as the review panels, which require a member of the leadership team from the home school and a member of the leadership team from the AP setting to meet on a regular basis with the teaching team at The Nest.

We developed the model as a result of a long-term piece of work around transitions for children with SEND and children experiencing crisis. We ask ourselves how the very best version would work for these children and families as they move in and out of the alternative provision. We then describe this to all the schools at the point of entry to them using alternative provision.

There are many conversations to make sure that everyone is clear about the expectations. We have a panel that meets on a regular basis that consistently returns to the terms of reference for our provision. We also discuss the other values that we hold between us and then ask how we make sure those play out in the decisions that we make about this particular child joining at this time. Those systems have held up relatively well and it means that whether you're in the trust or you are a local authority school, we work together to serve this community and meet the needs of these children and families. It's not perfect and it's not been easy, but it has held us to a level of expectation that we hold for ourselves collectively, which I think has meant that the children receive a joined-up approach to meet their needs.

I don't underestimate the amount of work to get that going, to have the systems in place and to maintain it. It's really impressive listening to you. And I just wondered what any of your young people say as a result of being part of this provision. What are the kinds of things they say to you?

Feedback from children and from families is one of the things that we hold dear. We talk with children in all our alternative provision settings on a regular basis to evaluate their learning journey with them and to talk about their choices and curriculum options. We look for anecdotal feedback from the young people all the time. We also have colleagues from special and mainstream provision who visit regularly, who talk with young people in order to glean a sense of what it's like to be a learner here. We've also carried out strategic pieces around storytellers and gathered views and video clips from children and adults across the trust. And we've tried really hard to make sure that we identify those young people to be part of those sort of pulse checks or videos or storytelling projects.

We have just created a film about attendance, and the children were just wonderful. One of the most powerful quotes from them was 'We would really like it if you talked. Don't talk at us. Talk with us,' and we thought this was so powerful.

In order to consolidate our work across our trust, we talk about great schools and making sure that within those great schools they meet needs. This is a shared accountability, shared responsibility, and it's the responsibility and trust that we hold for all those children across our community. There are many people who have contributed to the design of our alternative provision over time, and many have been instrumental in the way that it develops. It's definitely a shared responsibility; a collective endeavour.

Can you tell us about what you do nationally, because clearly people have recognised your expertise.

It's been a combination of luck and opportunity and connections. I am beating the drum for our most vulnerable children and being pretty resolute on making sure that they get the very best deal they can. That means that you end up connecting with people who are trying to do the same things. I think chairing the high needs working group is one of the things that has taken time and effort from a number of people. It has also felt like the antidote. We have moved on from finger-pointing to a place where we work on solutions.

We are focused on developing a system that's stronger for the future. I can look across the other four local authorities and see where things might be behind and where they might be ahead. And that has meant I have been able to do some joining up of the thinking and also align our work with the direction of travel in terms of the Green Paper moving into the White Paper.

I was then invited to be part of the DfE AP implementation steering group. That means I get the opportunity to be part of various networks and conferences. I've been involved with some of the Confederation of School Trusts' (CST) thinking around meeting the needs of children with SEND. There are also some brilliant publications available at the moment about the social model of disability, and it feels that there is a really strong narrative emerging: namely that it's essential that we recognise that this work is about children. This is not about children with SEND. This is about all children.

It has meant I have been able to have a say in the design for how AP might move forward. For example, what do we mean by digitisation of EHCPs? If we're going to move to that space, how do we look at the digital divide and make sure that our most vulnerable and disadvantaged families will be able to reap the benefits of digitisation?

Because of the different groups that I am involved in, I can see the ways that they intersect, but also that there is always a child at the centre of that, and therefore I can try to understand where we need to pivot, or lean, or exert moral influence or thinking to make sure that as we make these changes, they actually all line up in a way that benefits and advances the education for all the children in our communities rather than not.

It's truly impressive and very humbling listening to the determination and deliberate intention of the work, as well as the recognition of the uniqueness, the humanity of every child that you work with. Thank you.

Resilience, motivation, community spirit, respect, curiosity

A conversation with Laura Lawrence and Olivia Crutch

Laura Lawrence, deputy headteacher, and Olivia Crutch, head of primary, work at the Albright Education Centre, Sandwell's short provision for pupils with social, emotional and mental health (SEMH) needs and medical needs.

The Albright Centre works with young people:

- at their schools in Tipton (KS3–KS5) and in West Bromwich (KS1–KS3)
- at the bedside or in their classroom at Sandwell General Hospital
- in individual homes or virtually for home tuition.

Mary Myatt (MM): Tell us briefly about the Albright Education Centre.

Laura Lawrence (LL): Albright Education Centre is the SEMH and medical provision for Sandwell in the West Midlands. We take referrals for children from Year 1 up to post-16, and we teach across our centres in Tipton and West Bromwich, but also in Sandwell Hospital, and we teach children in the home. For home tuition, we either teach virtually or staff visit children in their homes. Our West Bromwich site caters for primary up to early KS3, with mixed-age classes. And then our base in Tipton is for KS3 pupils up to post-16. We are a short-stay provision. And we do lots of outreach work, particularly with our local teaching school hub.

MM: Tell us about the principles upon which you construct your curriculum.

Olivia Crutch (OC): When children come to us, each with a unique profile, there's often an unmet need that hasn't been identified. So, part of the principles underpinning our curriculum design is to build a curriculum that allows us to recognise and address the barriers that have previously obstructed the children's learning. We work with small mixed-age groups and help pupils to understand what learning looks like, as well as how they can become better at the act of learning.

LL: I think it's really important to start from the fact that our children come to us with such varied educational experiences. Usually, they've been out of education for a long time. We could have a child who comes to us with a broken leg who's not able to access their typical school provision at the moment, or we could have a child who has been dealing with severe anxiety and has been unable to leave the house, and is struggling to access education, from both a physical and a social perspective. So, you're shaping a curriculum around a huge breadth of ages and experiences.

We found ourselves doing a lot of work on baseline assessments for our children as they came to us. We looked at them from three areas of development: academic, school attendance, and social and emotional development. As we've gathered information about our children, over time five core values have emerged, which now underpin our whole curriculum: resilience, motivation, community spirit, respect and curiosity. These values are woven into their daily lives and are vital to them making good progress academically, improving their attendance and developing them socially and emotionally. And we know that those three areas of development are connected – if they are in school, they have a chance of making academic progress, and as they make better academic progress, they attend school more regularly, and as they attend and make good academic progress, they strengthen socially and emotionally. So those five core values have been shaped over time and underpin our focus upon the three areas for development.

OC: They are golden threads that run through the curriculum. Yesterday, we were trying to unpick what academic progress looks like, and we ended up coming back to the fact that academic progress depends upon resilience, motivation, community spirit, respect and curiosity. Our five values underpin any learning and form a base for all subject areas. Learners can only acquire more knowledge if they can adopt these skills. Additionally, they are a continuum: you can never be 100% resilient. You can always be more curious. We can look at a child and estimate how much more curious they have become, how much more motivation they have exhibited across all areas of learning. It's hard to judge, but those values are central to our children making progress in the three main areas of development across the curriculum.

LL: Any and all progress is progress for our children. Resilience or motivation or developing community spirit can look different for different children. We've created an environment for our children that ensures we capture all progress, and we celebrate that progress – whether that's walking into a classroom and engaging in a lesson, or just getting out of the car in the car park and taking that first step towards the building. We make sure that all progress is recognised by the whole school community and all of our staff.

MM: Okay. So, let's say you've got 'Michelle' who comes to you, and she is 13. What does her curriculum look like? How do resilience, motivation, community spirit, respect and curiosity manifest themselves when pupils are studying geography, history, RE, English, maths, etc.? What relationship is there between those five and the academic curriculum?

OC: Aged 13 is a good age for you to have picked! The KS3 curriculum is taught in mixed classes, which means that we can't spiral that curriculum at all. Therefore, we have to plan thematically, and we collaborate to make sure that children can make links across different subjects. For example, if they're studying propaganda in English, then that would be studied in history and art as well. We try to reinforce the big ideas by making them accessible in lots of different subjects. Then you come to our five values.

Take geography, for example, and the water cycle. We would teach the water cycle, but then we'd also be looking at each child's behaviour in that lesson. Are they curious? Do they ask us questions? How keen are they on going to the topic library, to discover more beyond what is being taught by the teacher? That's a measure of their motivation. Those are the traits we are looking for in lessons.

So, how do you make teaching resilience interesting? This is something that I asked myself when I first came to Albright. In my opinion, it needs to become intrinsic. And there's adult modelling of resilient behaviour within that. I will be explicit about it when a lesson is going to be about resilience. I might be teaching a group of pupils who are able mathematicians but lack the ability to bounce back after failing. So, I would have a lesson where I say explicitly, 'Okay, today I'm interested in you persevering at this problem. So, for you, what is that going to look like? Well, as with a real mathematician at university, who might be trying to establish a proof, you are going to successively fail now, over and over and over again. And that's because I want you to develop your ability to understand that failure is a part of learning. I know you find that difficult, but this lesson is about you getting better at that, not getting better at long multiplication.' Inevitably, those pupils will get better at long multiplication during that lesson and that will improve their social, emotional and mental health because they've achieved academically. But I draw attention to the fact that I'm looking at their resilience. I teach them that resilience is failing over and over again, and bouncing back every time. Another task might be to develop a better sense of community. For example, if pupils are learning about rivers in geography, I may ask them to gather snippets of information from other students or teachers around the centre to help them understand that it is beneficial to gather information from others in a team, or have the confidence to approach others to ask questions, rather than work as an individual. In this instance, the geographical knowledge would be no more important than the sense of community.

Ultimately, we can't escape that examination calendar. We want to challenge pupils to achieve the best they can. But when I first started at Albright, it was quite challenging for me to bring something like resilience to the fore. But one thing I've learned is that the pupils' academic development benefits greatly from investing time in building up those five values.

It's the same with respect. I'll explicitly say, 'Today, we are focusing on respect. So what does that look like? What do you think others may find disrespectful about some of your actions? How can you get better? Let's look for opportunities to be respectful and draw attention to it in a geography lesson... That was respectful because you showed compassion and empathy to someone else's way of life.' I remember a particular child who reflected on respect when we were looking at the refugee crisis last year. At the beginning of the topic, they were very much against people coming over in boats to this country, and at the end of the topic, they'd understood the reasons why somebody might want to do that, and why we should help. They reflected: 'I think that I've improved my respect.'

LL: I don't think it does us any good to brush the high level of challenge the children face under the carpet. I'll say to pupils, 'You know what? This *is* really hard. You're doing something that is tough. I know that what you're doing feels scary at the moment. It's really challenging for you, but you're doing it.' And we push through and build that resilience.

We do thematic days too, which are incredibly successful, where I see a lot of people teaching those skills explicitly. I think one of our key elements are our Wellbeing Journals, and I know, Olivia, because you're a form tutor, you've been using them successfully.

OC: The Wellbeing Journals, which children carry with them all the time, reinforce that idea that they are genuinely making progress in those five areas of resilience, motivation, community, respect and curiosity. When they start their Wellbeing Journals, they reflect on where they think they're at with each value. Then each day they consider how they have demonstrated these. At the end of each term, they self-assess to see whether they have become more respectful, feel more resilient, etc. I've had some children who at a certain assessment point seem to be getting worse. But, in reality, it was a reflection of them becoming more honest and saying, 'Actually, no, I said I could do that but I was lying a little bit, and what I've learned is, that I *do* find that hard, and I'll be open about that with you now.' Then we can look for a way forward. So that's been a really powerful tool.

This is where the pupils answer the questionnaire each term and reflect on their progress.

SEMH Questionnaire

Albright
Education Centre

Name.. Year Group.............. Date...............

Community spirit	Not at all	Some of the time	Most of the time	All of the time
I treat other people's belongings and the school with care - CS1				
I can work with other people - CS2				
I can talk to adults and other pupils politely - CS3				
I can include other people in a conversation - CS4				

Curiosity	Not at all	Some of the time	Most of the time	All of the time
I ask staff and pupils questions - C1				
I can listen to staff and pupils - C2				
I can choose a task to complete - C3				
I can share my interests and opinions about real-life events - C4				

Respect	Not at all	Some of the time	Most of the time	All of the time
I can follow staff instructions - R1				
I am able to share equipment with others - R2				
I understand which behaviours are acceptable and unacceptable - R3				
I understand other people's feelings and respond to them - R4				

Resilience	Not at all	Some of the time	Most of the time	All of the time
I can have a go at a task I don't like – RE1				
I can complete a task even if I make mistakes – RE2				
I know what might upset me and what makes me happy – RE3				
I can attempt tasks that are challenging or do things that might scare me – RE4				

Motivation	Not at all	Some of the time	Most of the time	All of the time
I can attempt tasks with support – M1				
I can attempt tasks independently – M2				
I can look for solutions to a problem – M3				
I attempt work that is more challenging – M4				

They colour the circle white, red, amber or green to reflect whether they have done something 'not at all', 'some of the time', 'most of the time' or 'all of the time' respectively.

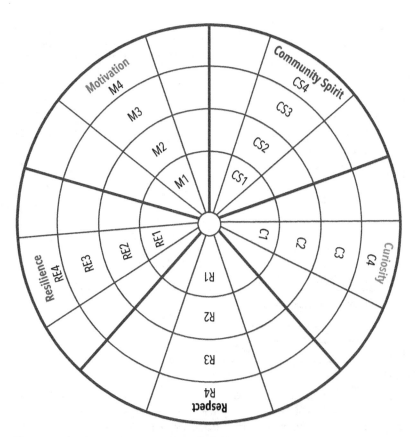

Then each day they record times when they have shown resilience, motivation, community spirit, curiosity or respect.

Week Commencing ....

Albright Education Centre

☹ ☹ 😐 🙂 😊 **Monday**   Uniform ☐   Equipment ☐

☹ ☹ 😐 🙂 😊

☹ ☹ 😐 🙂 😊 **Tuesday**   Uniform ☐   Equipment ☐

☹ ☹ 😐 🙂 😊

☹ ☹ 😐 🙂 😊 **Wednesday**   Uniform ☐   Equipment ☐

☹ ☹ 😐 🙂 😊

☹ ☹ 😐 🙂 😊 **Thursday**   Uniform ☐   Equipment ☐

☹ ☹ 😐 🙂 😊

☹ ☹ 😐 🙂 😊 **Friday**   Uniform ☐   Equipment ☐

☹ ☹ 😐 🙂 😊

Each week our primary pupils have an assembly focused on a particular value. Teachers then look out for how they are demonstrating it during the week and hand out certificates in next week's assembly called 'Wow Wednesday!'

And these are the equivalent documents for secondary pupils:

SEMH Questionnaire				Albright Education Centre

Name... Year Group.............. Date..............

Community spirit	Not at all	Some of the time	Most of the time	All of the time
I have respect for the school environment – CS1				
I can work as part of a group – CS2				
I can communicate appropriately when working in a group setting – CS3				
I can adapt to changes in the school routine and environment – CS4				
I am able to instigate and take part in appropriate conversation with peers – CS5				
I can socialise with peers outside my social circle – CS6				
I can change the conversation or introduce a new person to a conversation – CS7				
I can lead a group of peers – CS8				
Curiosity	Not at all	Some of the time	Most of the time	All of the time
I understand about people's personal space – C1				
I can listen effectively to staff and peers and understand social cues – C2				

Curiosity	Not at all	Some of the time	Most of the time	All of the time
I can have appropriate conversations and ask questions of peers/staff – C3				
I can respond to different social situations – C4				
I am able to communicate clearly and confidently – C5				
I understand how to interpret body language and facial expressions when engaging in conversation – C6				
I am able to have good eye contact with peers and staff – C7				
I can voice an opinion on real-life events – C8				

Respect	Not at all	Some of the time	Most of the time	All of the time
I can organise myself and equipment – R1				
I am able to follow directions and general expectations of staff – R2				
I am able to share equipment with others – R3				
I understand which behaviours are acceptable and unacceptable – R4				
I am able to talk to staff when I need to – R5				
I am able to behave respectfully towards staff and my peers – R6				
I am able to walk away from difficult situations and tell a member of staff – R7				
I understand other people's feelings and points of view – R8				

Resilience	Not at all	Some of the time	Most of the time	All of the time
I understand my own feelings – positive and negative – RE1				
I can express my own feelings – positively and negatively – RE2				
I am able to manage and reflect on my anxieties with support – RE3				
I am able to recognise when I am feeling anxious – RE4				
I can complete a task even if I make mistakes – RE5				
I am able to recognise and manage my triggers related to my anxieties with support – RE6				
I am able to manage and reflect on my anxieties independently – RE7				
I am able to recognise, reflect on and manage my triggers related to my anxieties independently – RE8				

Motivation	Not at all	Some of the time	Most of the time	All of the time
I can work with support to solve a problem – M1				
I can solve different types of problems independently – M2				
I can work as part of a group to solve a problem – M3				
I can identify a problem and work out the appropriate solution – M4				
I can complete my work without support – M5				

Resilience, motivation, community spirit, respect, curiosity

Motivation	Not at all	Some of the time	Most of the time	All of the time
I try my best when completing a task – M6				
I attempt the challenging questions in my learning – M7				
I am organised at home so I am ready for the day – M8				

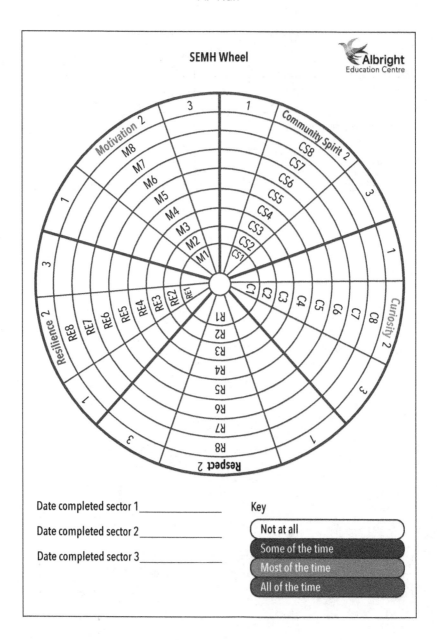

SEMH Wheel

Albright
Education Centre

Date completed sector 1_____

Date completed sector 2_____

Date completed sector 3_____

Key

Not at all

Some of the time

Most of the time

All of the time

MM: Quite often, mostly in primary, sometimes in early KS3 as well, skills are seen as though they float free, and they can be transferred without being located in the stuff of the curriculum. It appears that, in a very sophisticated and thoughtful way, you are linking skills development very closely to the curriculum experiences and what pupils are learning. It reminded me of John Kay's work on obliquity. He says that many goals are more likely to be achieved when pursued indirectly – *obliquely*. He says that if you want to lose weight, get more active rather than focusing on the losing of the pounds. You lose weight while being active. Coming back to your point about maths, Olivia… the explicit goal was to develop students' capacity to become more resilient, but they also got better at the mathematics. There's something quite interesting going on there, which is testament, I think, to the very imaginative way you have set this up. Without the kind of structures and the systematic thinking you've put into it, it could end up as something quite woolly, quite cosy, quite therapeutic, in a soft sense, not in a sort of true medical sense. But it seems the way you're delivering for your pupils has rigour.

OC: You're right. It's got the academic rigour as well as the focus on the five values. It's an effective combination. I think we'd be doing ourselves a disservice if we didn't admit to how much time and effort, and collaboration with subject specialists, goes into creating this structure. It also helps that we go from primary through to post-16. We're able to view the curriculum continuum. The bridge between primary and secondary is key because that is often where, for many children, it falls down, particularly with subjects like science. They can become very turned off when they move from Year 6 to Year 7. We're so fortunate that we can see the skills and the key knowledge they need across the phases.

MM: The professional development of staff must be a big element of your provision to be able to work across this wide age range.

LL: Definitely. We've always wanted staff to have mainstream school contacts as we take children from a huge range of local provisions. We want to have a finger on the pulse in terms of what's going on *outside* of our organisation. I want staff to be developing their own specialist interests because their passion is contagious. And I want them to be working on those five values as much as the children. Because the values are key for *people*, not just key for children and young people. I want passionate learners as adults so that they can model the five values to the children around them.

OC: Having deep subject knowledge is crucial too, as we just don't know what children have covered previously. We have to see who's in front of us and think to ourselves, 'Right, this is what you need to know now.' It's very difficult unless you have got good subject knowledge.

MM: Could you say a bit about the outreach work that you do with the schools…

LL: Of course. From an outreach perspective we work closely with our local teaching school hub. It's an opportunity to invite colleagues from mainstream or other alternative provisions into our setting. I always say to students and teachers or ECTs that I didn't know our setting existed when I was working in a mainstream school. I knew there was another 'place', but I didn't know what it was like, what it felt like, what it feels like to walk through the door of an alternative provision rather than a big, bustling mainstream, secondary or even a cosy primary school. So, we're keen to have people come to see what alternative provision is like. What does the day look like? Why are children here? And we've always said that ultimately *our* children are *your* children. They are the empty desk in your classroom. They're the child that your children are missing because they're poorly, and they can't come to school anymore. So, we really want to open our doors up so that people can come to see us and share our expertise.

OC: When I left mainstream, there were quite a few people who said, 'Oh, don't go into alternative provision. Don't stay there too long,' and I genuinely believe that at the moment my job is the real essence of teaching. It's holistic and I've learned so much more about pedagogy and spent more time thinking about how to improve my own teaching practice since working at Albright.

MM: When we interviewed him, John d'Abbro said, 'It's not a blame game, and I'm not criticising anybody. But mainstream isn't good enough for these children. Mainstream schools haven't got the capacity to do what we can do, because provision for these children has to be even better than what they would get in mainstream.' Alternative provision isn't the poor relative of the mainstream curriculum; it's actually the highest quality provision that these children need.

LL: We're in the borough of Sandwell. We've got children who come to us who live in Sandwell and could be accessing any of the Sandwell schools, but they could be in neighbouring borough schools as well. They just happen to live in Sandwell, but they might be in a Dudley school or a Birmingham school. We can't teach them exactly the same thing that they're being taught in their schools. For the children who are in the hospital or having home tuition, we're not providing the same intensity in terms of hours a week as their mainstream school setting. We can't match that. But developing a curriculum that is based on these five values really prepares them to be in their mainstream classroom or their specialist setting, or wherever they go to next. And we think that's key. We know that they're going back to specialists in their next setting, and they can pick up and run with a child that is willing to learn, ready to learn, engaged and curious about learning. They will absolutely be in their element. When they go back, they'll be with specialists again, and we see our job as getting them ready to be back in their forever school. We get them ready to be back in a learning environment with more children, and for a longer period of time; longer days in a bigger building. And that's why I think these five elements are so important. We know we have done our job when you get a pupil who says, 'Miss, would I be able to go back to my other school?' Or you can see them sat there going quiet, and they say, 'Hmm, I think I'm ready to give it another go.'

They mustn't be disadvantaged twice

A conversation with Katie Greenwood

Katie Greenwood is the outreach support team manager at the Stepping Stones School in Lancashire.

Please could you tell us a little bit about Stepping Stones and who you cater for?

We cater for children between five and 11 who come from quite a large geographical area of North Lancashire. We have feeds from the Lancaster area, Fylde and Wyre and the surrounding localities. We have two main groups of children. We have children who are permanently excluded, which is about half of our current population in the school, and then the other half of the children are on a short-term placement, which is a 12-week intervention placement. The goal for both cohorts is to reintegrate them back into mainstream education, if possible. We might be able to support a return to mainstream education, or it might be that alternatives are sought for them after they've had some time with us. At the moment we've got 31 children out of a possible 32 places. So we're relatively small for the area we cater for, which comprises well over 100 schools.

Tell us about your thinking behind how you construct the curriculum for the children that come to you.

All children have a right to an education, and for us all our children have a right to a mainstream education. So, we are fully committed to providing as many national curriculum opportunities as we can. Even with the children who are on a placement, their curriculum is built around the national curriculum. That said, we have a certain amount of flexibility in our approach. It's a rolling cycle, because our cohorts can look very, very different from one period of time to another. When we build our curriculum for the start of a new academic year, we will ask ourselves, 'Are these some of the areas we want to explore in geography within our school? Has this cohort already explored this? What might be a good direction to take them in?' For example, if we have a KS1 class that is working significantly below expectations, it might be that we choose a national curriculum topic that suits their needs better, rather than one that would traditionally be delivered to that particular age group.

Until recently, I led on the geography and history curriculum. When we built the curriculum, we looked at what experiences our children may not have had and what they might not have accessed previously. For example, in history we wanted to make sure that every year group had a balanced representation of historical figures, so we included history units on powerful women and issues around race. Being based in Lancaster, there's a significant link to the role that Lancaster played in the slave trade. And then we also try to make sure that we cover local history, things like the Pendle witch trials, which is really important because it's on our doorstep and we've got Lancaster Castle where a lot of the people were tried. We also ensure that we look at some bigger issues within the national curriculum focusing upon the UK as well as looking more globally.

We had a particular cohort in 2023 who were quite able Year 5s and Year 6s. And so when we designed their history curriculum, we really focused on the slave trade and crime and punishment element of our local history, because they were more able to understand the nuances of that particular curriculum.

Our younger children tend to be very practical, very hands-on children, and a sit-down curriculum wouldn't work for them. But that doesn't mean they don't access the same level of content. It's just delivered in a different way. So we devised a geography and history unit that focused on explorers, and they looked at female explorers, black and Asian explorers, modern explorers and past explorers. We had them building a ship outside, as they were going to go and explore the Antarctic! The history was delivered in a very practical way for them.

Geography is always a bit trickier for us. We believe in giving the children experience of their environment. We felt that the geography curriculum needed to reflect their locality. We wanted them to love where they live and feel rooted there, which for some of our children is very challenging, because they haven't had the best experiences of where they live. The challenge we've got with that is that they come from very different geographical areas. So, the geography curriculum is often based on where the children in your class are from at that time. So we've had one class, for example, where a third of the pupils were from Fleetwood, a third of the pupils were from Morecambe, and a third were from elsewhere. So, we compared the locality of Morecambe with the locality of Fleetwood, looked at the fishing industries in the two areas, looked at how tourism played a part in the past in how the two towns looked and how they've evolved and changed over time.

You have a massive amount of flexibility, then?

Yes, we have a vision. Our curriculum needs to re-engage our children with education. We need to make sure that any barriers to equal access in the school are overcome. So we design a curriculum that gives opportunities for successful outcomes; one that supports and encourages and has flexibility. We know we want to be flexible and creative and adaptive to the children's needs and their experiences. But it's got to be underpinned by cultural capital – those social, moral, British values. We want them to know their place in the world, because we're also very mindful that we are preparing our young people for the 'real' world, because, for our older ones, it won't be that long until they go on to high school. We do quite a lot of work with our older ones about what their aspirations are in life and what their path might look like to get there, if we've provided a broad and balanced curriculum, and if they've got more experience and understanding of the world. The curriculum links to possible futures for them, because sometimes some of our children perceive that they don't have a future, which is a very bleak thing to say, I know, but often many of the children we get are quite disenchanted with the education system.

So what do you do that engages them that the mainstream school couldn't do?

Well, the other part of our curriculum is the SEMH work we do; it's almost a 50-50 split. Our mornings are dedicated to English and maths. The rest of our days are split between our SEMH curriculum and the traditional foundation subjects of the national curriculum. We do a lot of work on values-based education that Neil Hawkes founded. That underpins everything we do. We have a very strong PSHE curriculum.

We do work linked to the Conscious Discipline movement that was founded by Dr Becky Bailey. We do a lot of work based around the zones of regulation, which seems to be increasing in popularity in mainstream schools. We do a lot of work based on class need as well because we've got that little bit of flexibility in our PSHE curriculum. We might have a particular cohort who really struggle to share resources. So, we might say, 'Right. Well, next week we're going to do a lesson on sharing, on the power of sharing, and on the impact of that.' We'll link it to the values we're doing that week. Recently, we found that our youngest pupils are struggling to let an adult work with another child. They automatically want that adult. By coincidence, our current value of the week is empathy. One of our teachers has written a lesson this week based around having empathy for others, understanding that everybody needs that time with the adult, and that creates a safe, calm classroom and ensures everybody gets a turn and gets their time, because everybody's waiting and being patient.

The other thing we always try to do is provide as many alternative learning opportunities as possible, too. Just recently we had a climbing wall delivered to our car park, and we have outdoor educational visits. Every term the children are taken to outdoor pursuit centres and that encourages both team building and that sense of achievement. Our motto as a school is that we are a 'can do' school – it's about the power of positivity. We do a lot of growth mindset work with our children, because they often come to us expecting to fail. They say they feel like a failure. Those extra opportunities are a practical way of practising the growth mindset rather than it just being a paperwork exercise or a verbal thing. You need to *feel* that success.

It's about finding dignity in positive things that they are successful at. Some of the dignity they find is being the toughest in the year group and just being so antisocial. That's where they get their dignity from. Tell us a little bit about the Neil Hawkes work.

So this is a bit of a passion project for me. Prior to coming here I was a teacher in a mainstream school. I was at one particular school for 10 years and I was instrumental in introducing the values-based education. It was something the headteacher wanted to explore, and I ran with it. I'd been the values leader there for a very long time, and I'm now the values leader here. So we have three core rules at school: we have the rule of respect, the rule of safety and the rule of learning. But those rules are very arbitrary if you don't understand what's behind them. So, we use the values curriculum that we follow to underpin that. Neil Hawkes created the values-based education movement and he identified 20 or more values that he felt children needed going out into the world. So things like trust, respect, understanding...

We've expanded the number of focus values recently, but when I came here, we didn't use all of them, because you need to really focus on what's most important for your context at that time. Our week will start with a values-based assembly where somebody will deliver to the children what the value is that week, and that is then explored all the way through the week. It's explored explicitly. We have a daily meeting where the children can nominate another child who has demonstrated the value of the week. The value is explored through English texts, through PSHE lessons, and other relevant aspects of the curriculum. It's about wanting our children to be the best version of themselves. For example, if you're focused on the value of 'trust', often those children who are a bit disengaged from the system will say, 'Well, nobody trusts me. Nobody thinks I can be trusted.' So we unpick that with them. And we get the children to see that all of these values have positives, and every child has those positives. You might hear an adult in our corridor saying, 'Oh, that's amazing. I'm so glad I can *trust* you to walk sensibly to the meeting room.' Something as simple as that little bit of praise has a great impact.

If I was working with 'naughty' children, I'd make sure I looked them in the eyes, and I'd say, 'I'm trusting you to do this.' It's really powerful. There's also a great line from Clive Stafford Smith, the civil rights lawyer. He's British, but he works a lot in the US with inmates on death row. I remember reading his 'This much I know' column in *The Observer*. He reflected on life and I think he quoted Seneca: 'It goes a long way towards making someone trustworthy if you trust them.' And taking that step over the trust precipice that you say you take with children... It's not a gamble. The more you trust people, the more it's an upward virtuous spiral.

I think that's what happens with our children. It's no reflection on their mainstream setting, because that has its own challenges, but they'll say to us, 'You listen to us, you *see* us.' We have the advantage of smaller class sizes. We have the ability to be with the children that little bit more. They are one child in 10 compared to one child in 30 in mainstream. It's about tuning in to the child and saying, 'I get this.' You know if one of our children is dysregulated or frustrated or upset, we never devalue that emotion. It's always, 'Yes, I would be upset. I would be frustrated, too. That's okay. What are we going to do to manage that?' We show understanding about how somebody else might feel. We show tolerance.

What's Conscious Discipline?

Conscious Discipline was introduced when I first started here. It's a movement by Dr Becky Bailey. It is centred around the idea of attunement. It's not dissimilar to the practice of emotional coaching. One of the practical tools that comes with it is 'Feeling Buddies'. They look like little gingerbread men, and they've all got different emotions attached to them. And there are eight of them, eight different emotions. You've got your core ones, such as happy and sad, and they have cousins, so sad's cousin is disappointment, and happy's cousin is calm. They link together. And you teach the children how to *feel* those emotions because what we found with the children at our school is that they're very good at naming emotions but have very limited understanding of what that emotion actually is.

Part of the programme is teaching children about the emotions. For example, you get out your 'angry doll' and you say, 'You know when you are angry your eyes might do this. Your face might do this, your body might do this.' And then you act it out physically for the children. They act it back to you so that they feel the physicality of the emotions. Conscious Discipline gave us a way to show the children we were attuning with them. We can say, 'I think you might be frustrated because your face is doing this, and because your body is doing this,' and sometimes they say, 'No, I'm not,' and sometimes they'll say, 'Yes, that is how I feel.' So it's a way of creating a very simple dialogue with the children. It ties in with creating calm spaces, which are regulation areas for the children to access.

For us, our main message as a school is that these children *can* do well. They are not written off when they come to us. It's a fresh start, a new experience for them, whether it's in a placement, or whether they've been permanently excluded. But we strive to give our children and our parents that high-quality, authentic educational experience. So, we put on Christmas plays. We invite parents in. We have parents' evenings. It's about inclusion within the education system. And yes, they're in an alternative provision, but they still have a right to have that inclusive education provided for them. They mustn't be disadvantaged twice.

The Inclusion way

A conversation with Julia Bray

Julia Bray is deputy headteacher at the Inclusion School where she is also responsible for the quality of education.

Please could you tell us a little bit about the Inclusion School and what you do there?

We are a new school that opened in September 2022. For the previous nine years, we were an AP supporting learners who were struggling to access the curriculum and schooling. Since opening as a school, we now specialise in supporting learners with mental health.

The Inclusion School is a mixed, independent specialist day school for children and young people with social, emotional and mental health needs (SEMH) aged 11–16. We enable young people who experience high anxiety, emotionally based school avoidance (EBSA), depression, suicide ideation and other complex needs, such as ASC (autism spectrum condition) and PDA (pathological demand avoidance), to access an enriching curriculum with bespoke learning pathways and qualifications in a safe, calm and nurturing environment.

All our learners have struggled with attending school, so they're all working below age-related expectations because they've missed a significant chunk of their education. This issue has been exacerbated due to COVID, and the demand for our services has significantly increased. We also have a college where learners can continue studying. But our aim is to prepare our learners to access a mainstream college once they've finished with us in Year 11.

What are the principles for curriculum design in your context for your children?

There are three things that underpin our curriculum. First, it's learner centred. Everything is based around what we can do to support our learners and help them succeed because they all experience poor mental health or have experienced poor mental health.

Second, it's about making sure that the curriculum is accessible, and third, that it's ambitious for the individual, because every single learner is at a slightly different point academically or pastorally. It's about making sure that everybody has the same opportunity, while personalising it to their bespoke needs, because all learners have an EHCP as well. Our key focus is mental health and emotionally based school avoidance. It's a very tight criterion for learners to attend. And we currently have 31 on roll. We have just recently had a successful Ofsted inspection, which allows us to increase our numbers up to 41. We want to remain quite small, deliberately.

We have to look at the cohort or the year group to make sure that not only can we meet the learners' needs academically, but also that they all gel as well. We teach the pupils in year groups. Now that's something that might change with time. At the moment, when you look at the personalities we have, the learners work well together. So that complements the curriculum because it enables us to make sure that we channel the pathways appropriately to their needs.

That is currently an average of five or six pupils per class. Do you have one teacher per year group? Or do you have subject specialists?

We have some specialists. But what we're doing at the moment is hiring primary-based teachers because we're plugging the gaps in the learners' knowledge. They need a primary specialist because the gaps are significant in their learning. But longer term, as these children stay with us and receive our therapeutic input, if they join us in Year 7, then in theory we'll be able to get them caught up to where they should be in the KS3 and KS4 curricula. Then we will explore hiring more specialist secondary teachers to make sure that our learners get the best possible curriculum and education they can.

Currently, in Years 10 and 11 we've just got young people who are so far behind, they are catching up to get to a level that is end of primary, early secondary at best. But if you've got some Year 7s who go all the way through with you, you'll end up with them taking a full suite of GCSEs, if possible, because they have had continuous provision, and you'd have caught them up with what they missed at primary. It's about that targeted intervention too and breaking down those barriers to learning.

So, what are those barriers?

We've got children with selective mutism who are now talking lots and flourishing, which is fantastic. We've got other learners who have dyslexia and just need that extra additional support. But then we've got other learners with significant gaps. It's about identifying that level of need, having the right assessment tools to support that identification and then monitoring it as we go along to make sure that we are keeping up with their needs.

How many teachers do you have?

We have about 10 teachers and several unqualified teachers who are doing their QTLS/Level 5 apprenticeships. All our teachers and support staff all teach and support throughout the day, with high cognitive demands in the morning, followed by our wellbeing subjects in the afternoon.

Our curriculum design is based now on a triangle model.

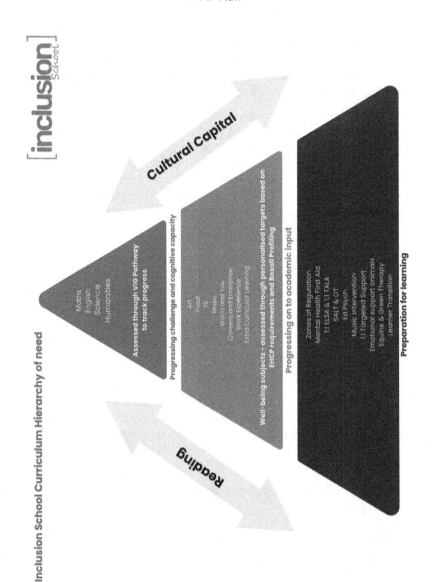

[inclusion] School

Inclusion School Curriculum Hierarchy of need

Cultural Capital

Reading

Maths
English
Science
Humanities

Assessed through ViG Pathway to track progress

Progressing challenge and cognitive capacity

Art
Food
PE
Music
World and You
Careers and Enterprise
Work Experience
Extra Curricular Learning

Well-being subjects – assessed through personalised targets based on EHCP requirements and Boxall Profiling

Progressing on to academic input

Zones of Regulation
Mental Health First Aid
1:1 ELSA & 1:1 TALA
SALT & OT
Ed Psych
Music Intervention
1:1 Targeted Support
Emotional support animals
Equine & Green Therapy
Learner Transition

Preparation for learning

The bottom of the curriculum triangle is all about mental health and making sure that the learners are ready to access their learning; making sure that the suitable therapies are available for our learners. And then the middle part of our curriculum is all about personal development and meeting EHCP targets. These subjects are food, art, careers and PE. The academic core is at the top of the triangle, which includes humanities.

We begin by establishing the mental capacity to study. One of the things that was noted by Ofsted as a particular strength was our building layout, and how we've made it a physical representation of what we're doing for our learners, because with our learners who have ASC, it's a logical approach for them. They know where they need to go if they need additional support and intervention.

We use a bespoke assessment platform for our learners to allow them all to achieve, as you can see in the following diagram.

Inclusion
Qualifications

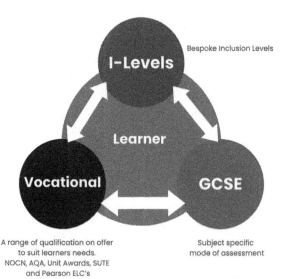

Bespoke Inclusion Levels

I-Levels

Learner

Vocational

GCSE

A range of qualification on offer
to suit learners needs.
NOCN, AQA, Unit Awards, SUTE
and Pearson ELC's

Subject specific
mode of assessment

We begin with our 'Inclusion' Levels. They're a bespoke level system we've created using KS2 and KS3 levels. They're our learning prerequisites before you reach GCSEs. They're statements that go from Levels 1 to 9, and once a learner has achieved all 9, we would look at progressing onto a vocational course or GCSEs. We've got I-Levels at the top because they are what we use to baseline our learners. However, learners may have a combination of pathways if deemed appropriate to their needs.

Please could you tell us in detail a descriptor of an I-Level.

So within English, we've got reading and writing and speaking. Our English teacher has gone through all the KS2 and KS3 requirements and defined very short statements that highlight when a learner reaches those requirements. We have done the same for maths. We break down all the skills they need to be able to achieve within that subject. But we then break them down between Levels 1 and 9. So if a learner is working at Level 1, we know that Levels 1 to 3 equate to Entry Level 1; Levels 3 to 6 tend to be about Entry Level 2, and then Levels 6 to 9 tend to be about Entry Level 3. It is a progression ladder for our learners.

Because our learners have missed so much of their education, it's very helpful, because it allows us to identify the gaps in their knowledge, and we then use platforms such as Star Maths and Star Reader to categorically identify roughly what level they're working at. So, in theory, we look at what the teacher is saying that learner is working at, and then we look at the tools that we're using, Star Reader and Star Maths, to see whether those judgements align.

Just to be clear. We're using the I-Levels as a diagnostic tool at this moment in time to identify where the gaps are and identify what we need to do next in terms of our planning because we've got some learners who have years' worth of education missing. We've just had a new learner join us who hasn't been in education for three and a half years. They were working below age-related expectations three years ago, and then they've had three years missing school; for that child, our I-Levels allow our staff to identify what's missing, methodically. I-Levels relate both to vocational and GCSE. They are generic. We've tried streamlining them as much as we can, and we know that this current model will be used for at least two years, but we will then look to develop it a little bit more over time, because we're not expecting our learners to all be on our levels if they've been with us for a period of time. The aim is that at the end of Year 11, each learner will receive a portfolio, a record of excellence, and they will either receive a portfolio of vocational qualifications that they've studied throughout Year 10 and Year 11, or their GCSE certificates and qualifications, or for our learners who haven't yet achieved those, they will receive an I-Level certificate, which is just as successful. If a learner gets those, if that's their benchmark, and if that's what they're working towards, and they've significantly improved during their time with us, then we celebrate their success just as much as we celebrate those who have vocational qualifications and GCSEs.

What's the importance of achievement for these children?

Oh, it's everything. It's the thing that builds their confidence; it's the thing that builds their resilience. And once you get that little bit of hope, and you make them realise that they can succeed, then it just snowballs, and by hosting an Entry Level 1 exam, our learners realise that they can succeed, and that they can do well, and then we have that time to prepare them emotionally for examinations because they've been outside of education for such a long period of time. It wasn't just a case of saying, 'Right, we're sitting some exams next week.' There was a lot of work that went into preparing them for those exams. It was a huge team effort, and by simply showing them that they could succeed, we've got happy engaged learners who had 0% attendance in their last school to, you know, anything from 70% to 100% currently. It has a significant impact on emotional wellbeing. It has a significant impact on attendance, and it has a huge impact on learners who might be struggling with selective mutism.

We've had a breakthrough this week with one particular learner who did not speak, who could not speak, and they are now speaking. They really struggled with interacting with other learners, with members of staff, and they've constantly got their hood up. Eye contact is non-existent as is speaking. Now this learner has selective mutism. And one of the things that I really dislike about that term is that there's nothing 'selective' about it.

This learner is paralysed with fear at the thought of having to speak. Now, one of the things that we do at Inclusion is that every day after lunch our learners are allocated a member of staff to read to or to read with and this particular student was paired with me, and I knew they weren't going to want to read out loud to me. So, I spent time just reading to them, and they just sat there, and they showed very little emotion, no response. But as time progressed, I started to get smiles. This learner started to sit up and I could see that they were starting to feel more confident.

And as time has progressed, we've gone from me reading the first page out loud, to them reading the second page in their head, and me reading the next page out loud, so we alternate. But you know, it's bespoke to that learner's needs. And then one day they spoke, and they said one word, and I thought, 'Oh, my goodness, don't celebrate, because that could cause more harm than good.' Then the next day I said, 'Oh, do you want to read that book? Should we go to the library?' They responded again, and I started to see these glimmers of verbal hope. And then last week I just got the book ready. And then I said, 'Oh, how are you? How's things?' And I said, 'Oh, I know you've enjoyed your lunch,' and I was answering for that learner. And then, all of a sudden, they started to talk, and we had 20 minutes of supported conversation. And they were able to tell me what it was that had stopped them from eating. They were able to tell me why they have worn their hood up for years, and they were able to tell me why they don't like speaking, and that was just absolutely amazing. And that's the power of reading.

Wow! Have you ever come across Gillian Clarke's poem called 'Miracle on St David's Day'?

No.

Oh, do read that, and find the version where she reads the poem aloud.

Yeah, absolutely. We will keep going, and we will keep developing that learner. But you know, considering that they've not been to school for years, that was a huge, huge achievement for them. But you just need to make sure you don't celebrate out loud, because the minute you celebrate or the minute you show a reaction, it can cause them to go back into that paralysed state. So, you've just got to pretend that it hasn't happened. It's about making sure that everything that goes on within the school, within the classroom and within the curriculum is suitable and accessible for all the learners and gives them opportunities to succeed.

We seek to understand how our learners are feeling before they enter the room. And so, with the help of specialists such as SALTs (speech and language therapists), OTs (occupational therapists) and education psychologists, we've created a task plan process, and these are available for every single learner, every single lesson. Initially, they will identify what zone they're in because we're trying to get the learners to think about how they're feeling and why they're feeling that way now. They don't have to discuss why they're feeling that way. They just simply need to identify. Now, if we've got some learners who can talk about their emotions, then we will touch upon that throughout the lesson on a one-to-one basis, but it just gives the teacher the ability to understand where they are, in terms of being ready to learn.

	What Zone are you in?		
BLUE	GREEN	YELLOW	RED

The Big Question.....

1.	Put electronics away	☐
2.		☐
3.		☐
4.		☐
5.		☐
6.	AFL Trays/ Incluros	☐

Check Out:	What Zone are you in?		
BLUE	GREEN	YELLOW	RED

To begin with, rather than having a learning intention, we have the Big Question, which is accessible to everybody in the room. But it's really important that when staff are designing a Big Question they use certain phraseology, like, 'How can I turn a solid into a liquid?' If they were to use the words, 'Can I...?' then, instantly, you're providing the opportunity for a learner to shut down and say, 'No,' or if they have autism, 'No, I can't.' And then you're done for! So, it's important that, with the Big Question, we think really methodically about the knowledge that we want to unpick in that lesson. Ideally, we want the learners to be in the green zone. But we know that their mood can vary each lesson, and it could be triggered by the transition from one room to another, or it could be interacting with others. It could be the subject. But the task plan process helps us to identify and then understand where that learner is when they come in, and also it allows us to then communicate with our mental health lead or engagement team if we feel that that learner needs additional support, so we can get somebody else in the room quickly. We can do it without causing a scene. It's about having a rapid response when we feel that that learner needs support, whether that's in the classroom, or whether they need to come out of the classroom.

Imagine I'm one of your learners. I'm in the green zone, maybe a bit yellow. The Big Question goes up on the board. What happens?

So, we have the acronym IDEA, which stands for identify, describe, explain, analyse. They are learning progression steps. It doesn't matter if a learner only gets to I or if somebody else can achieve all four; they've all achieved part of the Big Question. It allows us to show progression into the next lesson and identify where we are and what we do next on our task plan. If you notice to the right of the form, we've got boxes where learners can indicate how they feel about that stage of that learning by either ticking or colouring in red, yellow, green or blue. What we're working towards is an activity that's low threat, high challenge, so they want to be there, and they're engaged.

We then begin to challenge them to see where they are on the IDEA continuum. We would then finish off with our assessment for learning trays to end the lesson. We have traffic light trays, red to yellow to green, based on how you feel that you've done in the lesson. 'Can you please put your work in the appropriate tray?' For some of our learners with selective mutism, it might be that they choose their tray, and they feel happy because they don't have to speak. For some of our more confident learners, I might say, 'Well done. You've put it in the green tray. Can you tell me why?' But then for others, who really don't like making those decisions and who don't like feeling that they've got to explain, I'll simply say, 'Oh, I think you're between green and yellow. As you go out, could you just put your book into whichever tray you think it is?' It's about teaching the learners every single lesson to identify their emotions as well as take part in the lesson, as well as to evaluate how they think they've done in that lesson. So, once they've popped their work in the assessment for learning trays, we then have Incluros. They're our inclusion coins, and the learners take one of those and they pop it in the reward bucket. Once they have filled a bucket, they get to choose their trip. At the moment they've chosen bowling. But again, we are not organising that. They know that if that box is full, they have to call the bowling alley. They have to get the trip booked. They have to do it. So it's about embedding those basic life skills by putting the ownership on them, which works really well because we have Student Council regularly.

And then at the end of the lesson they can just check out blue, green, yellow or red, and if anybody were to identify that they're feeling red and they're not feeling great, it just gives the teacher the opportunity to inform the next teacher before they get to their lesson.

So, red is angry. Green is fine. Blue is sad and yellow is not sure?

Absolutely that. We use the code in every single lesson. We use it in every single conversation. We have a 45-minute lesson, followed by a 10-minute break every single hour, which supports regulation and decompression time. This is complemented by having an open-plan building with multiple kitchens. Learners can get themselves food and drink and take time to regulate and decompress after lessons.

The following displays are in every room and most communal areas of the school for students to write on, and these also help support the process of regulation:

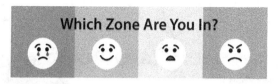

Angry

Frustrated   Scared

Sometimes cry
you might walk away

Zones of Regulation

Happy

Focussed   Ready to learn

yippee   absolutely
"yes maybe"   fantastic
you get good sleep   smile
chilled

Worried

Confused   nervous

withdrawn

Tired

Sad   bored   Unwell   Neutral

grumpy   I am tired

not listening or
not focussing

We can't have a bell, so we've just installed a tannoy system to remind the learners where they need to be, because a lot of our learners can't tell the time. Despite being so significantly low in terms of their age-related expectations (they're definitely secondary learners with primary academic ability), the key thing is that they want to be treated like adults. And that's why we call them 'learners'. We don't call them 'pupils'. We don't call them 'students'. It's key. If we were to call them students or pupils, their retort would be, 'No, I'm a learner.'

With regards to marking, we've had to go to a primary model, because that's what our learners remember. That's a positive experience for them. It's about trying to pick out what's positive for our learners, and then making sure that we build upon that. We provide verbal feedback every single lesson and we see the impact of that in the progress evidenced in their books. Our marking sticker is an A4 sheet where we write 'Star Moments'.

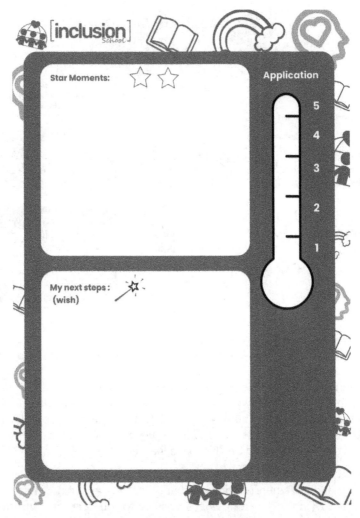

As long as there are more positives than negatives, it doesn't matter. We ask the learners to colour in on the thermometer how well they think they've been doing within that topic. This is done *with* the learner, not *for* the learner. We do this in the middle of a topic to reinforce positively the progress they're making, and to say, 'Do you know what? Well done! You're doing this really, really well!' But then we must always link to the next step in the learning. 'So, what are we going to do next?' We're saying to the learner, 'This is what we've achieved. This is what we're now going to do to push you further.'

So we've got verbal feedback every single lesson, and we've got the marking sticker. In the last week of every half-term, learners will complete the reflection sheet.

Reflection Sheet

This topic, I have been learning about:	

At the start of this topic, this is how confident I felt about my knowledge surrounding _____ :	

During this topic, I have learnt:	

At the end of this topic, this is how confident I feel about my knowledge surrounding _____ :	

Teacher Review (Linking to your subject 'wish/EBI's'):	

They identify on the emojis where they felt they were at the beginning of the topic. And then, 'during this topic' they go through, independently, the Big Questions they've tackled and identify what they've learned. They then identify how they feel now. We should be able to track their progress. The aim of this is to show them how fabulous they've been, and show them how far they've come, because a few months ago they weren't leaving their bedroom. They weren't coming into school, and their attendance is now significantly improved.

And then the teacher review should always link to the 'Wish' or 'Even Better If', so that we've closed the loop before we go on to the next topic.

Incredibly well structured, incredibly thoughtful, student centric and achievement centric, while consistently using a trauma-informed approach. It's prioritising the academic. But with all the support they need to get really intelligently structured curriculum structure and qualification structure. How do you prepare them to leave and go on to the next stage of their learning?

We have a strong work experience/transition programme embedded within our curriculum. Every Monday, our Year 11s go to work at the Wellington Country Park. They do the same on a Thursday. We focus on developing their skills for employment. They develop a centre of excellence portfolio. They take with them a CV, a set of core skills and everything that they've learned, so we can then help them make an informed decision when it comes to the next stage of their learning. We're not ready for GCSEs this year, but we've become a GCSE centre. Staff are being trained as examiners. We want to be ready in case we get learners through the door tomorrow that can do GCSEs.

You know what, they love being at school. They absolutely love coming to school, and it's the only school I've ever worked in where every single learner loves to be there. It's hard to get them to leave!

It's *main*-stream, not *all*-stream

A conversation with Jess Mahdavi-Gladwell

Jess Mahdavi-Gladwell is the deputy headteacher at Robson House, an alternative provision facility in Camden.

Please could you tell us how you got into the world of AP?

I had always been really motivated by those children who didn't manage well. When a SENDCO position in a secondary pupil referral unit came up, I decided to have a go. I really enjoyed that, and I think the SENDCO role prepared me well for moving into more senior leadership. I applied for this post earlier than I'd anticipated, but it was quite clear, within about 10 minutes of me walking into the building, that this was the place I wanted to be for the next chunk of my career. I'd worked in one primary school that had a base unit for children with learning disabilities and social, emotional and mental health needs, and another that had a nurture provision, but I'd never worked in a primary that was wholly for children who hadn't managed in mainstream.

Tell us a bit about Robson House.

Robson House has a maximum of 20 children. Because we are designated as a pupil referral unit, they're not allowed to come to us until their fifth birthday. So that means, on occasion, a child's fifth birthday present is to join us. They have to move on at the end of Year 6, at that usual secondary transition age. Children come to us at varied times in between, and children stay for varying lengths of time.

The referral process in Camden is through a joint panel for children who have been excluded or are at risk of exclusion. Children referred through SEND, who have EHCPs, are also considered at the same panel.

So we've got, I think, a high number of children with SEND, even though we are deemed a PRU. We always have more boys than girls, but we do have some girls. And I think on the whole, children who have floundered in mainstream come to us.

Imagine one of those children who comes in on their fifth birthday and they finish on the last day of Year 6. When they leave at the end of Year 6, what would success look like, if you had taught them a really rich, ambitious, challenging curriculum?

That would wholly depend on the child. You know, we have children who don't have a diagnosed need, and we have children who do. What I find really interesting about us is how we group our children based on their developmental stage rather than purely chronological age. That said, we try to keep our Year 6 pupils separate because they have a really robust transition programme. But beyond that we could have a Year 3 child in the same class as a reception child, or a Year 2 child in the same class as a Year 5 child.

I think fundamentally what success would look like is that they've learned how to learn, that they understand not knowing something isn't failing. Our job is to teach them – that's why we're there. If they knew it all, then what would be the point? Often, the first thing that they have to learn is that adults can be trusted, and school is safe. Many of them haven't experienced school as being welcoming and psychologically safe. Often the experiences of children who just don't fit the mainstream mould are that schools don't feel safe, and sometimes, they've not even been in schools where they've been safe. I'm not criticising our mainstream colleagues. We know they do what they can with what they're given.

You know, some of our children leave before Year 6. They do a period of work with us, and then we get them back into mainstream before that secondary transition. Some of them end up in special provision at secondary or sooner. Some of them go into mainstream with lots of support, and some with less support, because they don't need it anymore.

And some of them go to the secondary pupil referral unit. There's a wide range of outcomes. And I think we do our very best to seek the right setting for each child, and then to do everything that we can to support them to be in that setting and to be successful there.

Tell us about the range of issues that your children have that means they're with you and not in mainstream.

I think most of them just can't cope with being in a classroom with the teacher–pupil ratios in mainstream classrooms. They find it hard to manage the demands of mainstream classrooms and the level of sensory input they face. Some of them have ADHD. Some of them do have a diagnosis of autism, though if autism was their primary presenting need, they probably wouldn't end up with us.

Their needs in mainstream tend to be described by those wonderful words like 'defiant' and 'disruptive' and 'aggressive', when, actually, they're just struggling. And some children, when they struggle, become very withdrawn. Some children when they struggle present in a very different way, and I guess the PRU generally gets the children who have been described in those really negative, deficit terms. I don't know if you've seen that wonderful poem called 'Why am I rude?' circulated on social media recently? It's great. It's a whole bunch of children and young people explaining that perceived rudeness, talking about the underlying reasons why they react as they do... 'I'm hungry. I didn't have any clean clothes. I didn't understand what you meant.'

And many children in PRUs and alternative provisions have language needs, but they've learned to mask them. They've learned to not be vulnerable. So, they present as being able to understand fully what they've heard. They appear to be refusing to follow those instructions where actually, you know, their language needs mean that they might have heard the first thing that you said, possibly the second, maybe the last. They absolutely can't hold those things in their heads and sequence them, and some of them have learned coping strategies that are effective for them. But repeating things aloud to help them to understand doesn't really work in a class of 30 children.

So, a child is described as too noisy, too disruptive, not getting on with other children. Well, you know, if you've got an underlying need of autism that leaves you with a deficit in terms of theory of mind, well, you're not going to get on with other children. You might not see the point. You might not understand that you've hurt someone's feelings or offended someone. There are lots and lots of reasons why children say and do the wrong thing, and I think it's rarely because they've decided to annoy an adult.

When we interviewed people for the SEND book, we were clearly talking about SEND and not talking about alternative provision. Now we are interviewing people about alternative provision, there's suddenly an overlap. What you're saying is, I think, that if you have autism and you are not coping in mainstream, it's a fine line between going to a special school or going to a PRU.
It just depends. It just depends how they react to that environment.

If you become insular and withdrawn you might go into a special school; if you come out fighting and react physically and abusively, you might end up in a PRU, and you'll be described in deficit terms. Is that a fair overview?
It's quite a generalisation, but I think it's a generalisation that probably fits lots of children. You know, there are all those other things that feed into it, like do their families have enough readily available money to feed them? Are they warm? Does their situation at home mean that they have a calm adult at home in the morning who can focus on helping them or not? In my experience, there's probably less of that in primary. When I worked in secondary there was an awful lot more influence from things like child sexual exploitation and child criminal exploitation and county lines, and you would see children who had been very successful, and

who were very academically able, where something had gone wrong, and that had led to them doing something inappropriate. If you look at the national picture, the older children are – even if they should be in a special school – the less likely they are to have access to a safe space.

So, it is a complicated picture, but every day I am reminded of my firm belief that no child behaves in a way that is not acceptable to adults or atypical or not mainstream, just because they've decided to. They do what they can and when they can't, that's when it becomes hard to manage. When you've got one teacher, maybe one teaching assistant, 30 children, no break-out space, no soft room, no mentoring team, no team of adults whose job it is to communicate with families and build those relationships with schools… Sometimes, when you're an adult working in alternative provision, part of your job is to rebuild the parents' trust in the education system as well as the child's. If you're working in a system where there just isn't that wider support provision, it's tough. You know, we know how many hours our teachers work, and we know that teachers aren't social workers… I think our children need somewhere with more capacity.

Graham Nuthall said in his book, *The Hidden Lives of Learners*, that the education system is not set up for learning. If you want children to learn something, you wouldn't put them in classes of 30. But we're educating the masses, at scale, on less and less money in really difficult times. And it's hard. But it's not a blame game. So, tell me how you organise the curriculum, because you talked about it being in development stage groupings up to Year 5, not in year groups. Tell me how that works and tell me how you structured the curriculum. What's the experience for them in the classrooms? What are they taught? What do they learn?

If I think about our youngest class, a lot of what they do is very Early Years Foundation Stage in style. They need regular breaks or changes of activity. We start with their interests. We have to work wholly on relationships. The first thing that happens when a child comes is that we take some time getting to know them, *really* getting to know them – not a quick, half an hour chat – but really getting to know how they interact, what works for them, what their triggers are.

And we want to know those little individual things that can snap them out of being in a really grumpy mood, or that sense of how I am going to help this child to move away from the Red Zone, if we think about our zones of regulation. Sometimes it's just something really silly. I remember a few months ago playing peekaboo through a window with a child in Bulgarian, and he went from being incredibly angry to being ready to go back into class in such a short period of time. As adults in a setting like this, we've got to be prepared to try things that might make us look a bit silly and might not work. By doing that we can build a picture of what that child is like, honing our sense of knowing that child. That means that we can spot their triggers at the earliest stages.

We're a small school so we can alter our curriculum. If we're due to read this book, and this book is all about a little boy and his mum, and you know you've got a little boy in your class who doesn't live with his mum, and that's a really recent thing, and he really struggles with it, you can change the book. We don't count break and lunchtime as not-learning time. It's just different learning time. If you look at our curriculum, which was co-created by some members of my team and the previous senior leader who led on curriculum, we've got physical and emotional wellbeing in there, communication, language and social behaviour learning, and behaviour and citizenship. And then, underpinning things, we have growth mindset and mindfulness, and the really thorough work that's done on zones of regulation and helping pupils to learn to recognise and understand those negative feelings in themselves so that they can then begin to recognise those feelings when they're small before they get really big.

Obviously, there's lots of work around all of those things in what you might call traditional lesson time, but also at playtime, where we focus on lots of positive interaction in playing with the children. The value of playing with the children is recognised.

They then have mentoring sessions, which can follow a kind of general-ish curriculum, but also can be really tuned into what that child needs at that particular time, whether that be something to do with an interaction with a peer or something that's going on in their life outside school.

Every minute that they're in school is an opportunity for us to teach them something. And we do have a really varied academic curriculum. They learn computing, they learn RE, they have a French lesson taught by a French specialist. We have a music specialist in. I had an architect come in last week because one of the children was interested in architecture. He came in and did this amazing presentation for the children, which was actually really quite wonderfully linked to their interests. He really pitched it well, thinking about what they would be interested in, how he could hook them in.

I think one thing it requires of us is to be brave. So, we took all our children to the ballet a few weeks ago and on the day, in the morning, I was thinking, 'This was a crazy idea!' And most of them loved it, and some of them didn't really enjoy it, but they all now know if they liked it or not. I think we're lucky to have easy access to lots of truly enriching things. We work hard to make the most of the cultural capital on our doorstep.

You said that if you're successful in your setting the children would learn how to learn. Could you talk a little more about that?

I think one thing that is hugely important is to tell them explicitly, and then also model, that getting something wrong doesn't mean you've failed. Getting something wrong merely means, 'Well, we've now got an opportunity for you to learn how to do that correctly.' We all make mistakes and most of the time nothing bad happens, apart from you might feel a bit silly. Actually, adults sometimes feel a bit silly too about not knowing something; I'll say to my children that sometimes not knowing something or getting something wrong is really uncomfortable, and if I get something wrong, I might feel a bit upset, or I might be a bit grumpy. And it's okay to feel all of those things, and then we need to try a different way of approaching what we've got wrong so that we can understand how to do it right.

How do you convince them of that? Could you give a tangible example? You could give us a specific example obviously without naming anyone.

Somewhere I've worked before, I had a lovely maths teacher and a wonderful pupil who was convinced that they couldn't do maths. 'I can't do maths. I don't do maths. There's no point in trying to get me to go into the maths lesson. I'm not doing it. It's pointless.' And this teacher, who was a trainee teacher, broke the maths learning down into tiny chunks. Ever so slowly, she spent a few minutes a day doing maths with this pupil. She would come in for three minutes for a tiny nugget of maths, and then the next day and then the next day. She gradually increased the time. Over several months, she created a batch of work where the learning was such tiny steps that the child could experience that sense of progression in a really gentle and safe way. The teacher was able to hook in other key adults to know about this pack of work, and they encouraged the child to access it. At the time it felt like it was taking forever. But within six months we had a kid saying to me, 'Let's do maths now!' and absolutely desperate to take home the sheets with 50 correct questions. *But*, if there were 49 correct questions and one wrong, it wasn't a big deal anymore, and it was all because that teacher was determined to see that barrier as a challenge rather than an obstacle, and then thought creatively to get around it. She was prepared to be flexible, prepared to put in some extra time and effort. All those things happened because the relationship came first.

If you can enable a child or a young person to trust you and then explain something in a way that they can understand, and do that from a position of knowing them, knowing their needs, knowing their barriers – all of those things that are very difficult in mainstream settings with large classrooms and less than ideal ratios – then they can start to believe you. And for a smaller child, that sense of success can sometimes happen through play.

Sometimes it's – as an adult – being prepared to pretend that you couldn't do it and then letting them correct you, and about not having that concern – 'Are they going to think I've lost face and lose all respect for me?' I do think it can require out-of-the-box thinking and actually real, genuine bravery as well as being a skilled and knowledgeable teacher in terms of subject knowledge or pedagogy.

What you're saying is you have to get to know the child deeply. You have to create a safe space for them to learn and *safety* is really, really important. And then because they are in such a safe place in your institution, they can breathe out and the pressure lifts from them. And

the pressure they felt in mainstream – through no fault of anybody's – is suddenly alleviated and they can be themselves and relax. And then they learn.

Yes. Something I've said enough times that anyone who sees me regularly is very bored of, is that it's called **main**-stream, not **all**-stream. I thrived in a mainstream setting, and so did most of my peer group. And when I look at children and young people in my family, most of them are thriving in mainstream and most of their peer groups have, and I think when you work in alternative provision, or in a special school, you can kind of lose sight of the fact that mainstream's great for most children, but just not all of them.

You said that Year 6 are in a single-age group because you've got a detailed transition process into secondary provision. Tell us about that and how that works.

Well, we know early in the academic year where our Year 6s are going, so one of our mentors is focused on the transition programme. So, they look at what the travel route's going to be. Is the child going to get transport, or will they need to learn how to do this journey on their own? They also look at what children find difficult. So, some children are good at getting up in the morning, they find it really easy, and for some children it's much more challenging. Some children don't really have a problem sorting out a morning routine where they get up, get dressed, clean their teeth, eat breakfast and pack their bag either the night before or in the morning. But some children just don't have the well-developed executive function for those things, so the team will create lists or visuals, and they'll know what's going to work for each child. Some of our children, even when they are even eight or nine, they'll say, 'Don't put pictures on it. I'm not a baby.' And some of them need the pictures. Some of them need, as I said, more help than others, or more help with different things, and again, that knowledge of what the child finds easy or difficult, what support is already in place, what work has already been done and what they're going to need to learn to do, is key.

And then working with the child, with the family, and also with the next setting, we ensure we have really effective communication about the child's strengths and barriers, what the school's expectations are, what can be considered a reasonable adjustment, and what the school's hard boundaries are. It's happening at the moment; I notice things like regular discussions about deodorant, showering in the morning versus showering at night, packing your bag at night rather than packing your bag in the morning. What kinds of things might you need in your next school that you don't need to think about yet? We have to prepare them for uniform, because we don't have a uniform. One thing that's really important is we have a year-round programme; we have activities through the holidays where children can come with their families, they don't come by themselves, and we allow our children and their families to access things that parents might be a bit worried about – how to handle those people who can give you the look in public if your child's misbehaving or make an unwanted unnecessary comment. And so, because we do things with a group with our lovely, experienced staff, the children get to experience success at those things. It builds families' confidence that their children can do these things.

That means that we don't have the children drop off a cliff in July. We continue to work with them through the summer, and then we continue that work for the first few weeks or months of secondary, depending on how they settle. It's lovely because sometimes they come back. You know we've had a couple pop back, one who recently moved on to secondary, and one who's all grown up and working. It was mighty lovely to see them come back and want to share their successes with somewhere they knew had had a positive impact on them. It's so moving to hear how we've created such a brilliant, safe culture for the children who need the best possible provision.

A forensic approach to the curriculum

A conversation with Lucy Holloway

Lucy Holloway is the deputy director of education at Wave Multi-Academy Trust.

We are a trust across the southwest of England, Devon and Cornwall. We have 11 alternative provision academies. One is a special school, two are medical alternative provision academies and the remainder are for pupils permanently excluded or at risk of exclusion from mainstream provision across the region. We have about 1000 pupils and students in the trust across both primary and secondary. In the alternative provision academies, the aim is that they stay with us for two to three terms, but the reality is that it can often be longer.

My background is in mainstream where I was part of the senior leadership team in a large secondary mainstream provision before coming into AP. What I love about alternative provision is that we are able as educational professionals to reach those pupils that were often more difficult to reach when I was teaching in mainstream. It's in alternative provision that I believe we can really make a difference. Initially my focus was on English, and my focus is now on the whole curriculum across the trust.

I'm starting off by talking about the academic element of our curriculum in AP. We really make sure that our curriculum is doing what it needs to do. Why does teaching this matter? Why have we prioritised this piece of learning in the sense of knowledge, understanding and skills at this time for these individual pupils? We constantly need to evaluate the curriculum through the lens of our children and young people who receive it; to whom it is their daily bread and butter. Because if we are teaching X, we are not teaching Y, and every second counts in alternative provision. This is where we are often the last chance to make the difference in whether pupils re-engage with learning or not. Many of our pupils have turned from it to date, so we need to be utterly 'intentional' about what it is we are trying to do here.

So, when we think about our taught curriculum, not only do we need to be clear about why we are teaching what we are teaching in the curriculum design, but we also need to have the highest expectations of our young people. That's why we have said 'we will teach humanities' and 'we will develop the most expert teams of reading teachers that we possibly can' and 'we will teach English literature'. Because if we do not open eyes, hearts and minds to the world, it may be the last chance at this in an educational setting. That is real. That's a responsibility. I think that background in both mainstream and in alternative provision gives me a good insight into the curriculum and what is possible. This needs to be combined with an empathetic understanding of the difficulties that many of our young people face. The best-resourced curriculum in the world isn't going to land if pupils are not yet in the right place and the reason they have not managed in mainstream to date has not been effectively identified and supported. So meeting pupils where they are is a constant part of our work in AP. And we need to be equally mindful of our goal of preparing our young people, either for their return to mainstream education or their next steps.

Another factor so critical in building the academic aspect of our curriculum in alternative provision is ensuring we support and develop teacher subject knowledge where needed. Teachers in our small settings often need to teach out of subject specialism in secondary, so we need to support this. We've said we want humanities on the curriculum, but it may be a maths specialist delivering this, so we have ensured our humanities curriculum is there to support, and we train through external partnerships. An example is a scheme of learning we commissioned through the Associate Research School and ex humanities county advisor on 'Who deserves a statue?' More about this later. The fact that we have secondary subject specialists in the same provision as primary can be a strength when developing the curriculum. We have developed teacher subject networks and it's helpful that these can be offered online, particularly for colleagues who are subject specialists working on their own. It's important that we facilitate our solo subject leads to get together to develop curriculum and pedagogy.

We don't want to be a 'mini mainstream' in terms of the academic part of our curriculum, but equally we need to make sure that while our curriculum is alternative, it is also 'provision'. The question is how to marry the two elements, and I believe that we can have these great expectations of our young people. It means that we are very forensic about what we select to teach. This matters, because this might be the last chance for some of our young people to receive a proper education.

We have to be thoughtful and what has been helpful about the Education Inspection Framework (EIF) is that it has encouraged us to be intentional about the diet we provide. We regard it as the gift of curriculum – what it is we're going to give our young people – and we need to be utterly precise in our intent. This also provides some flex, but we must continue to be very clear about what we're teaching and why we're teaching.

We consider the national curriculum documents, and we pull through the golden threads that we believe are particularly important in AP. This is because, unlike mainstream, we have pupils stepping in and out at different phases and with gaps in their learning. Equally, they often have untapped schemas of knowledge, and teachers need to make sure that they are not making assumptions about gaps. This means that assessment is important for us because it gives teachers a forensic starting point for where to pitch the curriculum.

In primary, we prioritise the teaching of reading, and I'm sure every school would say that, but for our pupils it is essential. We collaborate with the local DfE English hub to help us ensure that we're doing it as well as we possibly can. When we look at a subject like history, we are mindful to consider what comes next so that we can prepare our pupils to return to mainstream.

In terms of history, for example, our aim is for our young people to be able to ask questions, to think critically about the past to understand the present and to identify bias. However, we cannot teach the whole of the history national curriculum because we don't have time, and our priority in the school day is often beyond the academic curriculum, where we are supporting pupils with social learning or delivering the more vocational aspects, which are so vital in AP. We think it is important to do fewer things in greater depth. So we alternate between geography and history in primary and in KS3 to make room. We keep the subjects distinct and don't dumb down. We consider what will be useful in their future learning across a two-year curriculum. We decide on our important 'non-negotiable big ideas' like 'parliamentary democracy' and 'experiences of migration' and thread this so that pupils joining us at completely different stages can develop their understanding, rather than repeat work from mainstream.

We strip it back and select elements that we believe will be interesting for our pupils. For example, 'Why did young people join the Hitler youth?' We also teach about Vietnam and ask why America was fighting there. This brings a wealth of opportunity to look at the world order today. Taught expertly, pupils value this and are naturally interested and curious. Taught from Twinkl, less so. So that goes back to what I was saying about giving teachers the time, resources and support. They have to really 'understand the intent to be able to flex to reach it'. That's a bit of a mantra. Another thread of our history curriculum relates to experiences of migration. This work links to our trust's values of inclusion, respect and empathy, and we ask ourselves where we teach these across the subjects.

In another history unit we ask who deserves a statue and we explore issues of representation through history – for example, the Plymouth footballer Jack Leslie, the first black player to be called up for England. We investigate why he was dropped from the team sheet, and we link this to the Edward Colston statue. We also learn about Mary Anning, and we try to support our young people to link these historical figures to their locality, and at the same time to look beyond these to wider issues of diversity and inequality that resonate today.

We want our pupils to understand the concepts of power and protest over time, which draws in causation and consequence. We want them to gain an understanding of the experience of minority groups throughout history. We spiral these themes through the topics. This means that those pupils who are stepping in and out at different times are not missing out. Every unit needs to work as a standalone unit as well as be threaded with big themes of time and a sense of place. This is because pupils join and leave at different times, so that is an extra nuance for our curriculum design.

We also consider the chronological knowledge and awareness that our pupils need, and we make sure that at the start of each half-termly topic we have that timeline up in the classroom, and we're able to show where this topic sits in the timeline. We make a point of asking pupils, many of whom might be new to the school, what they already know about what has happened in the 20th century. Do they know when something took place and what happened before and after? This is a sensitive way of doing some assessment. Assessment can be difficult in AP when pupils have just joined and you stick a test in front of them. It's not always going to be the most conducive way to finding what you need to know, so assessment for us is critical and planned well into the curriculum.

Sometimes in alternative provision there can be an apparent tension between the need to have a 'planned' curriculum with the broader aspects of our work in the sector and supporting our pupils to get back on track. And because sometimes so much of the work in AP is 'unplannable' given the context and difficulties many of our young people face before they have even set foot in the door, it is complex. And sometimes, when we began this work in our trust, conversations around assessment and curriculum could be met with some fear that because it was now on paper, this meant it 'had to be delivered'. Or that having a set curriculum would prevent teachers being able to respond to pupils' motivations/interests in art, for example. Or that doing English literature GCSE would switch pupils off. Taught well, it is the opposite. Pupil voice tells us many pupils love keeping up with their mainstream friends studying GCSEs, which is part of our 'core offer' at Wave. Or there may have been a perception that a focus on academic curriculum learning was at odds with therapeutic learning in art, for example. I think we are through that now, and we believe that the curriculum should be both therapeutic and academic. For example, in art there is the capacity for it to be therapeutic. However, it is equally important to teach pupils how to get better at art so that they have a voice and develop the skills to be able to express themselves. Some of our art network articulate this brilliantly and it helps us move forward.

This goes back to the tension, I think, between learning of the curriculum – or studying for GCSEs – and the purpose of AP where for some of our pupils we initially need to focus on personal development. We need to prioritise that. We need to be clear that if we're going to change these people's lives for the better, we need to do it through education. As a school, we need to be providing the highest quality of education. So it's about being absolutely clear on what the priority is for that young person at this time. That's the challenge for our leaders.

How does the curriculum work at KS4?

We have a core offer, and we aim for our pupils to be entered for at least five Level 2 or higher qualifications, and they achieve some excellent results. We offer English, English literature, maths and science at GCSE level in all our AP academies. Pupils tell us that they enjoy discussing English literature with their peers. We believe this means that they are still included with their peers in mainstream.

We also offer functional skills, Level 1 and Level 2, which are a backup or a bridge for further study. We also provide BTECs, which are site specific. The vocational learning is important and also sometimes more difficult to provide as we don't have the same facilities as mainstream. It means that our schools are innovative and work within their regions to offer what's available. For example, one of the APs offers small animal care, where students spend a day a week at the local zoo. This is so powerful in terms of the wider aspects of the social and personal development curriculum.

We also have links with local post-16 providers and colleges, and we find that that vocational element has to be quite bespoke. We are also developing unit awards. These are entry-level qualifications. They are helpful because they cover a range of studies. For example, one teacher is offering a unit award on the basics of a guitar, preparing meals for a family of four on a budget, sewing a cushion, etc. I think that will be a growth area for us in the future because these can be delivered within half-termly blocks with a tangible outcome, which is pretty powerful for pupils who are with us for short periods before going back into mainstream, and it enables curriculum breadth. The awards often provide a sense of belief. We also run BTECs in personal growth and wellbeing, sport, work skills, IT and the introductory award. Our leaders are dynamic in seeking these opportunities.

We believe that if we are going to change pupils' lives for the better, then one of the ways we will do that is through qualifications as outlined. But we also recognise that there are some young people who need extra pastoral support. We know that we are not going to get to the academic bit until that has been sorted. This is another reason why our academic curriculum must be razor sharp and precisely planned in order to enable the space in the timetable for teachers to attend to pupils' social skills and broader development.

To support the development of social skills, we use a 'readiness for integration' tracker. This helps in assessing the specific barriers to learning and engagement and for finding ways to overcome these both across the curriculum and through enrichment opportunities. We look to marry the therapeutic elements with the academic provision. And the timetable and curriculum need to be able to flex for timescaled packages/pathways for individuals at the appropriate time.

Our enrichment curriculum is pivotal to our offer for young people. We want pupils to develop a sense of leadership as well as their social skills. For example, we may need to help some of our pupils to be aware of their impact on other people when they are in public and be able to cope in unfamiliar settings, such as museums they may never have been to. The enrichment sessions are structured, so that pupils are not just going off and having a nice time, but learning and applying skills, as well as reflecting and planning. (Though having a nice time is still part of our intent!) We want pupils to enjoy *and* achieve, not just achieve. Like reading!

It is underpinned by a very intentional personal development aspect, so that when they visit a museum, for example, they are not just learning about the artefacts but also reflecting on their ability to interact with other people. We need to get our pupils out of the bubble of AP. We are intentional about providing an offer – both on the pastoral and academic fronts – that aims to hit the sweet spot of high challenge and low threat. And we have some incredibly super skilled staff here.

In summary, working on the curriculum design in alternative provision is a lesson in the importance of working backwards as curriculum thinkers. What are the outcomes we need and want for our young people? How will teaching X support this? What will this look like through the eyes of our pupils experiencing this?

It's a lesson in the importance of training your staff who may be working beyond their trained specialism in delivering the broader curriculum.

It's a lesson in the importance of marrying two potentially contradictory concepts: being well planned/laser intentional and being flexible/adaptable. And supporting leaders and teachers to get this balance right so that empathy never becomes 'ruinous' or expectations of what our young people are capable of as learners and thinkers are never compromised.

It's a lesson in being outward facing and internally growing, so that across our 11 schools, solutions and innovations are celebrated and we draw in external expertise to help us grow too.

I don't think we are ever 'done'. But I like that.

The curriculum: plane flight or bus journey?

A conversation with Alison Woosey

Alison Woosey is the director of educational standards at
Bolton Impact Trust.

In my role I spend time talking about the curriculum with colleagues and
plenty of time in lessons talking to children. It's a lovely role. I worked
originally as a teacher in the trust. I taught in mainstream for 10 years and
then left to have a baby, and I didn't want to go back to work straight
away. But then an opportunity arose in a young mothers' unit, and I
tiptoed back into the world of teaching again, with my little one!

I've stayed at the same trust with various roles to the point I am at now.
The Bolton Impact Trust serves Bolton schools within the local authority
and other local authorities in the Northwest and it works with about 200
young people. There's primary provision – the Forwards Centre – where
we work with primary-aged children who have been excluded (or are in
danger of being excluded) from schools in Bolton. There is also Lever
Park for pupils who have needs identified within an education, health
and care plan relating to social, emotional and mental health issues. We
also have Youth Challenge for secondary-aged children who have been
excluded (or are at risk of being excluded), and Park School, our medical

provision for pupils who are not able to attend mainstream school for medical reasons. We also teach pupils who are in Bolton Hospital.

How do you think about the curriculum for your children with a wide range of both needs and starting points?

The job is to meet children at the differing points in their curriculum journey and to plan for that. It used to be the case that APs would aim to fill the gaps and to just squeeze education into them before they left us. What was missing was thinking about the curriculum journey they had already experienced, and we didn't think enough about sequencing the curriculum, for example. I think we've come a long way in recent years, and there's now some nuanced thinking about the curriculum for pupils in AP.

I find it helpful to compare the curriculum in mainstream schools to a plane flight. The curriculum in mainstream can be planned, and pupils encounter the milestones over the key stages to a destination at the end. In alternative provision, it's more like a bus route. We have a beginning and an end, and we plan for that. However, there are many stops in between, and pupils can get on and off the 'bus' at any moment. This means that the quality of the journey is massively important. It might be a one-stop shop journey, or it might turn into a lengthy journey. This means it is crucial that we plan that whole route well and sequence it carefully. The short stops need to be well planned and sequenced as well. We've got to give our pupils a rich experience, for however long they're with us.

When they get off the bus and hopefully return to mainstream or another setting, we aim for them to be able to join and leave at any moment, and this is through a knowledge-rich curriculum.

That's a very helpful way of framing the curriculum for young people in AP. How do you go about planning for this?

When we are planning for the medium term, we make sure that the distance between the two stops is very rich and is not dependent on previous stops. It means that pupils get a solid experience of a topic in depth, and we plan the topics in a cycle. This means for pupils staying with us for more than three terms will revisit the same concepts but at a deeper level. The units are underpinned by a degree of repetition and knowledge retrieval. Pupils are able to hop on and hop off depending on the length of time they are with us because the sequence is cyclical rather than going towards a single endpoint.

For example, identity is a theme that we look at in autumn because identity is huge for our children; they often come to us quite confused about who they are and have quite often been rejected for who they are and how they behave. We explore identity with them, and we do this through a lot of the subjects, including English, humanities and PSHE. We aim for the theme to be interwoven across the subjects so that their depth of knowledge, experience and understanding are likely to be more coherent.

We talk about our curriculum beginning at the door; when the children come in, our curriculum begins. This means that personal development is an important element of the curriculum in our settings. It's important that we get this right, because many of our children are with us for a short time. We don't believe it is appropriate to plan subjects in isolation. The themes we choose for each term are intended to tie the learning together.

We check how things are going and I visit classrooms on a regular basis. I had a lovely example recently in PSHE where pupils were learning about the stages of grief. I was in an English lesson later, and I asked one pupil about the novel they were reading. She said that the young girl in the novel had lost her father and was having a lot of problems. The pupil went on to say that they understood grief better because they had been learning about it previously in PSHE. It meant that they were able to make the links and to deepen their understanding.

We're ambitious for our children, and we believe that they deserve that. They also need people to advocate for them and to be ambitious in the curriculum they receive. This is one of the reasons why we consider identity and link it to ambition, because pupils will often tell us that they don't believe that they can achieve great things in the future.

We have five strands that link to the trust's values, and we weave these through the curriculum. The strands are knowledge, character, creativity, innovative thinking and transforming potential into long, lasting success. This means that while we make sure that the curriculum is knowledge rich, we are also asking how we can build character through maths, humanities and vocational studies, for example. We ask ourselves, what skills are we giving them for life? What barriers are we aiming to remove so that our pupils can either go back to mainstream and be successful, or go into the world and be successful?

Sometimes this means considering the pace of the teaching, rather than making the content easier. We had one young man with us whose behaviour was very good. When the CEO of our trust asked him why he had been excluded, because he was working hard and doing well, he responded that it had just been too fast for him in his mainstream school. What we take from this is that we can still provide a knowledge-rich curriculum, and if it is delivered at the right pace, it can be attainable for our pupils.

At KS4 we make a point of teaching about finances so that they are confident understanding wage slips and discounts when they are shopping. We think carefully about what our young people need to know to be successful in life.

Pupils take GCSE courses where appropriate and also BTECs. The vocational studies are important for our young people. We find that they are able to see the point of learning when they realise where the qualifications can take them. We have a separate personal development curriculum, which includes careers, and this runs through from KS3 to KS4. We also make sure we tap into their interests. For example, any pupil with a passion for music is able to take a qualification. We also had a pupil in the medical provision who achieved a top grade in Latin GCSE! In order to make this work, we have very good links with the mainstream schools, which are underpinned by collaboration between the settings.

We enrich the provision with plenty of opportunities; we arrange visits and have visitors into the settings. For example, the Forwards Centre for primary-aged pupils have the Forwards Centre 40 entitlement, which means they have great experiences across the years. We find that these experiences often reignite their interest in learning.

How do you think about professional development for the staff in your settings?

Professional development is very important to the trust, particularly working on the curriculum since the different providers came together as a trust. We work together and we also link with mainstream colleagues so that we can draw on their expertise. We allow colleagues to personalise their learning where they select from a suite of sessions, and we find that this gives them ownership of the process.

For example, I ran a curriculum conversation session last week, and we are doing feedback and retrieval questioning next week. We find that colleagues identify an area where they want to improve, and we make sure that support is available. Our colleagues are very enthusiastic about their professional learning.

I think it's fair to say that we don't think we will ever be in a position where we say we have finished our work on the curriculum; it's an ongoing piece of work.

A CEO's perspective

A conversation with Debra Rutley

Debra Rutley is a National Leader of Education, and Aspire has grown in both size and impact under her leadership. Debra has taken on a new alternative provision unit each year since 2012, all five of which have now been judged as 'outstanding' by Ofsted.

I've been in alternative provision for 23 years. I previously worked in mainstream as an RE specialist and I also taught some English. I moved into AP as a deputy head and then became a headteacher. As we grew the provision and the number of schools, I became the CEO of the Aspire Schools Trust, where we have about 240 young people on roll at any given time.

I decided to work in AP because they were the children who would be drawn to me in mainstream. I would often have the classes that other people didn't want. It just felt natural to move with some of the students into alternative provision, and everything I do, I think, is a result of the experiences I had in school myself. I really identify with the young people in AP: I am dyslexic, I came from a poor background and I think I was probably classed as a failure at school. I see myself in these children and I want to offer them better opportunities than those I had in a mainstream school.

It is interesting how we feel called to do certain work, isn't it? And it doesn't mean it's an easy path, but there are deep rewards when we work with vulnerable young people. Could you tell us more about the Aspire schools?

We have three types of provision. We have the typical PRU provision for children who are excluded from school and SEMH provision for children with EHCPs, which is more nurture based. We also have SCM (structured clinical management) provision for children with mental health challenges. We also provide education for children who are physically unwell and who are either at home or in the hospital.

How do you and your colleagues think about the curriculum provision for those three areas of need that you support?

We don't have one size that fits all. It's very different and bespoke within the different areas. We have three words underpinning our curriculum: safe, love, learn.

What we mean by this is asking ourselves these three questions: do children know how to keep themselves safe? Do they feel loved? And have we created the conditions so they can learn?

Love is interesting, and I don't think we talk about love enough in the sector, either professionally for one another or for our children. I think it would be good if love were mentioned more often. I think it's powerful that love is your second value. How did you come to choose that?

I talk about love all the time, and particularly in our AP settings, because sometimes children present themselves as 'unlovable'. They are the ones who need our love the most. I will say to staff, 'Is that good enough for my child? Are we treating them with love? Because they are going to learn with and through love.' Young people know if you want them to be in your classroom; they know if you're excited to be working with them. They can see that, and they feel that. And then they respond to that love. It's not pink and fluffy, because it can be a really hard value to live by.

It's lovely to hear you talk about love. And then I particularly wanted to pick out 'to learn'. What struck me when I visited one of your schools was that you had very demanding and high expectations for the students.

I think what you will hear in most alternative provision is that the key is relationships. And that's where the love comes in – ensuring children know we see them as valuable human beings. What some of the children tell us when they come into alternative provision – particularly children with mental health and medical needs – is that people don't see them. They say, 'Teachers and leaders in schools don't see me.' What we do at Aspire is say, 'I see you. I notice you.' That's the start of the relationship.

It's also about the children valuing themselves. They need to be able to say, 'I have value and worth, because you see me and you know and care about me. You want to talk to me. You're interested in me, and you're preparing lessons and telling me I can do this and helping me to do this.' It's like creating a new identity that says, 'You're worthy and valuable as a young person.'

In terms of the curriculum at KS4, students follow GCSEs or BTECs. At KS3 our number one aim is to help them to return to mainstream school. We are working on a new curriculum – 'Finding my Voice' – which is a deep personal development curriculum offer. What we're trying to do is to give children the skills to go back into mainstream school with a new sense of self as a valuable human being, and where they see themselves as learners.

We want them to be able to communicate what they need to be successful in school rather than communicating by kicking off and walking out or not attending. We believe you've got a right to be at school, and if it's not working for you, there are ways and means in which you can communicate that.

'Finding my Voice' is a 12-week full-time programme with six strands. It's about transforming self through love. It's our intention that children become empowered readers. Books are at the heart of our KS3 curriculum. They learn about themselves and we look to develop creative confidence through problem solving. We also work on emotional literacy so that they are able to say, 'I'm not in a good place today,' or 'This is what happened to me.' It means that they learn to be aware of their own emotions and are able to name them.

We also have a strand called 'powerful purpose'. This is about providing opportunities for children to ask themselves, 'Where am I going in my life? What ambition do I have for myself?' And the final one is 'finding my voice', which is about being able to articulate ideas and emotions clearly. This is a new piece of work, and it has been challenging, both for staff and students. It works on a primary model and there are plenty of opportunities for talking with a real focus on developing relationships.

We also work alongside the mainstream schools. Colleagues from mainstream come to see what we're doing, so that the children are going back into a supportive environment.

The main thing about designing the curriculum in alternative provision is that you have to be prepared to change it to meet the needs of the children who are in front of you. You can't sit in the room and design something fabulous, and then say, 'Well, these aren't the children I want! These children don't fit my curriculum.' We have to respond and adapt to the children.

We have to do something different, and offering the same diet as they had in mainstream that wasn't working for them meant that we threw it all up in the air and started thinking that if we have 12 weeks with these young people, what do they really need?

Beyond the core of English, maths and science, we also offer arts and languages, so that the children can continue with their studies from school. When we are supporting children who are being educated at home, we liaise closely with the mainstream schools. We aim to support them so that they are not falling behind. And it's really important if you're not well enough to do a full week of the curriculum that you can get to study stuff that you like! If you're not very well, and suppose your favourite subject is Spanish, if we were to say, 'No, we don't teach Spanish, sorry about that,' it would be a shame. It means that we have a bank of tutors, and we're always recruiting and making sure that children have opportunities to study the subjects they love.

I think the most important thing about the curriculum provision is that it is designed to flex, to help the young people realise that they can actually learn. They might not be very good at this at the moment. The way we think about this is 'Let's tap into what you're really good at and interested in. This means we can transfer those skills across to other areas of learning.' We aim to develop curiosity and if every young person left with the capacity to be curious, that would be amazing.

The placements are generally for 12 weeks at KS3, which is quite a tight turnaround, yet if they were to stay with us longer, there's a danger they could get comfortable. For the most part, it takes about a term for the young person to transition in and out of the respective settings. At the end of the placement, there's a graduation ceremony to celebrate their achievements.

In terms of the enrichment provision, we try to create opportunities for children that they wouldn't normally have. That can range from camping trips to the seaside or going to a book shop. We had developed a good relationship with the Youth Hostel Association who are able to meet the needs of the children. We believe it's important to know the children and also know what extra activities are going to benefit them.

Sometimes it's just about going back to play, which they might have missed out on. If, for instance, a young person has been a young carer, it means they will have missed out on a lot of their childhood. It's not play therapy. It's just a child playing because they have missed out because they've been responsible at a young age. And I think that when we talk about plugging gaps in education, we tend to talk about teaching children their times tables, but sometimes it's about teaching how to play and have fun. For example, our mental health provision is situated in the woods and on a Friday afternoon they all play manhunt!

It's the greatest gift we can develop in our young people, isn't it? Can you tell us about the training put in place to support professional learning for your staff? It would be good to hear how you manage all this with adults in terms of the curriculum and curriculum changes combined with meeting the needs of all the young people that come to you.

We have to invest deeply in our staff because they are the ones working with students all the time. We do a great deal of CPD relating to trauma practices and all our provision is based on nurture principles. This means that we make it explicit that you belong in the school, and you feel as though you belong, whether you are an adult or young person.

We have plenty of opportunities for departments to meet across the different sites. We believe in raising the bar in terms of professional development for teachers working in alternative provision. We are involved with the Princes Teaching Institute[1] for subject-specific development, not only engaging with the subject-specific CPD, but also contributing to the programmes, for example, in science. It means that our colleagues are contributing to high-end conversations about the curriculum. And this is important because it's about having high expectations for your staff as well as your pupils.

---

1   www.ptieducation.org/

The landscape for pupils in hospital education

A conversation with Cath Kitchen

Cath Kitchen is the chair of the National Association for Hospital Education.

Can you tell us how you came into the field of hospital education?

I was the mother of a child who was in hospital education. At that time, hospital provision could not open unless there was a teacher present. When a teacher was off sick, my daughter piped up, 'My mum's a teacher, she'll come and help out!' That was how it started. When the statutory guidance for medical needs and hospital education changed in 2000 with the publication of the first statutory guidance, 'Access to Education', a job was advertised in the local hospital school. I started as a teacher on the ward in the mornings and teaching in homes in the afternoon. Later I became the headteacher and went on to create The Skylark Partnership, a MAT of two schools, the first multi-academy trust for hospital schools, where I became the CEO.

I retired just over a year ago. However, I continue my role in promoting children's rights, to ensure equal access to education for young people in hospital, through my role as the chair of the National Association for Hospital Education. I co-chair the Hospital Education Working Group at the Department for Education, and we're looking at how the proposed changes in the Green Paper will have an impact on our children and our sector. I'm a member of the AP Stakeholder Reference Group and part of the AP SEND Green Paper implementation group. I have not left the sector, because that is where my heart sits. I meet amazing children who drive you on to make a difference.

Having been a parent of a very unwell child, I know that you don't have the capacity to fight for your child's right to education because you are just worried about their illness. I feel very strongly that it's up to us as professionals in this sector to be able to do that for our children.

Do we have the headline figures for the number of young people receiving hospital education?

No, the DfE does not hold that information. A few years ago, we did a freedom of information request to every local authority to get some sort of idea, and I did do a little bit of a breakdown, looking at what education provision each local authority was offering their children with medical needs. As hospital education comes under the alternative provision umbrella, it is difficult to get an accurate number because each local authority has evolved its own system for meeting its Section 19 duties to provide education for children with medical needs. There are only 12 designated hospital schools across England, the definition of which is a 'special school that is contained within a hospital'. However, this does not cover all large hospital schools, such as in Nottingham. This is classed as alternative provision yet comprises a large regional hospital school, a CAMHS unit and a medical alternative provision unit. Provision has evolved differently across different local authorities. Hospital education, in its widest sense, is either education that takes place on a hospital ward (this can be a paediatric hospital or a child and adolescent mental health unit), or there might be young people whose state of health prevents them from going to school but who do not require hospitalisation, whose needs are met in the community within medical AP. Some local authorities have a home tuition service included.

The home tuition services are not registered. This means that they're not inspected in the same way: the good ones invite peer collaboration and have robust quality assurance processes, including school improvement partners. However, this is not universal, and a child's education becomes a postcode lottery. A regional hospital, such as Great Ormond Street Hospital School, which takes children from all over the country, discharges children back to their home local authority. If they are fortunate the local authority might provide up to 25 hours of support. If they return to a local authority that provides home tutoring or online tutoring, it might be as little as an hour or a few hours a week. It seems unbelievable that in 2024 where you live determines the quality and the number of hours of education that you get if you are unwell.

NAHE was involved in advising on the update to the statutory guidance, and the lawyers removed most of what we said because we wanted 'must' instead of 'should'. As it stands, the statutory guidance says 'as much education as the child can manage, equivalent to mainstream peers'. This means that it is open to interpretation. Of course, there are some children who can only manage an hour a week, but that doesn't mean an hour a week for a year, with no review. A child might start with an hour a week, and when they're able to manage that, we should be asking whether we should put in another half hour or more. It's about constantly reviewing, in the same way as for any child on a part-time timetable. It's not a destination. It's not the end point. It's part of an intervention to support them, to recover and to be able to access full-time education again.

I think for children, it's like having a double whammy. If a child gets a serious illness, and for some, their illnesses are life limiting, that's bad enough to cope with. But the fact that you might be behind and not be able to move on, it's as though you're being penalised twice for something that is outside of your control. It doesn't sit right.

There's a further issue in that we don't have any sophistication in the coding for registers. This means that if a school has a child who's really unwell, and goes for kidney dialysis on a regular basis, once a week they'll get 'M' for medical appointment, or 'I' for ill. But there's no subtlety in that, so it is impossible to tell whether this a complex and enduring illness or not. If you were to ask the Department for Education how many children there are in the country at the moment with complex illnesses, they don't know the answer, and the only way to do it is by digging through NHS data, which is also quite difficult.

It was a key step forward that alternative provision was included in the Green Paper, and it meant I was able to be the voice of the children in hospital education through all the uncertainty of the pandemic and from that collaborative work with the Department for Education. It's enabled AP to be treated as part of the whole SEND system. It means that we've gone from being the poor relations to being able to take a place at the table alongside the solution for children with SEND. When the discussions about the proposals and pilots are taking place, it means I can make sure that pupils in hospital education are also considered, and I have written a paper about why the DfE needs to look at hospital education separately from alternative provision. That was how the Hospital Education Working Group was created.

I believe that you can opt to be part of a solution and use your expertise and knowledge to support the DfE, who don't have the expertise and knowledge, to be able to develop something that will make a difference for our children. We now have work streams of practitioners in our sector, defining exactly what hospital education is – and, just as importantly, what it is not – on key performance indicators that are relevant for us. For example, if we consider a regional hospital that discharges children to different local authorities, having reintegration rates as one of its key performance indicators is inappropriate as it has got no control over what goes on when the child goes home.

We are looking at how we support schools currently in what the Green Paper calls the 'tier one' outreach model and collating what we're already doing to support schools to include children with medical needs. We're looking at what the Section 19 duty and what the school finance duty say, and trying to pull something together to help colleagues at the DfE come up with a sustainable funding model, because a school has no control over which children are admitted to hospital. A school doesn't opt for a child to go into hospital in the way they do for other alternative provision. There isn't any choice. You need a basic number of staff to open a hospital school, whether there are two patients or 30 patients in bed. It's different from the commissioned model that exists in medical AP or the home tuition service.

If we can come to a tight definition, then the question becomes whether we can look at different ways of funding it. The bottom line is that the hospital inpatients need something different from medical AP. There are some cases such as the Sheffield Hospital School, which has a medical AP as part of their hospital school. They have key performance indicators (KPIs) that they report back to their local authority as part of the commissioning arrangements. It means that we have this example and other local commissioning arrangements that we can draw on. Hospitals are also inspected by the Care Quality Commission (CQC) and inpatient CAMHS provision is inspected by the CQC and the Quality Network of Inpatient CAMHS (QNIC), which has two pages on education standards.

Currently there are different systems, and we believe that we might have the skills and expertise to pull something coherent together. It means we would be able to offer advice, for example, on the proposed Progress 5 measures developed by the Fisher Family Trust as a possibility for AP. We believe that if we develop something from the sector that we're already using to judge the quality of provision, then we are more likely to increase the standards of what is being offered to children. If we have meaningful measures, rather than trying to shoehorn things into a set of KPIs that don't suit our sector, they will be more meaningful for our children.

How is the curriculum framed for individual children in this part of the sector?

There is variability within the hospital school sector. Professionals are skilled at including outside specialists and many provide an enriched curriculum by bringing in, for example, music. Some of the sports and PE that takes place on the hospital wards is honestly absolutely stunning! It might mean working with physiotherapists and occupational therapists to deliver this aspect, while always being mindful that the intention is that the child will return to their home school.

It's very important that the pathway is designed so that they keep up with their work because children get very anxious, after a period in hospital, about returning to school. They worry about whether they haven't kept up and if their friends have moved on. There is work to counteract the social isolation that can happen in a hospital when teaching the academic curriculum. It means having opportunities for children to come together (perhaps not for maths and English, though the pupils might all have the same starter for maths), and then they will go off and do independent work. However, the music or the PSHE can be done collectively as a group, or it might be the case that the older children read with the younger children.

There are plenty of opportunities and it's important to be flexible. If a child is not very well on a certain day, you might ask whether they would like to be read to. Children tell us that it's an opportunity to forget about their illness and be a normal child. It's also an opportunity for those children who are in for a short stay to find out, for example, what might be worrying them in maths and for us to provide a lesson in that. This can have a big impact for the child when they return to their home school. In medical AP, we might get children who have missed most of Year 10, but still want to follow their Year 11 studies, and we are very skilled at teaching GCSEs in a year.

There is also an opportunity to bring in British values through rich discussions in English and other subjects. When a child has been isolated and out of school, away from their peers, they can miss out on the opportunity to have these conversations. While we never diminish the academic element of provision, we also need to take account of the impact of the illness and consequent social isolation. For some of our children, like the children who've been excluded, they feel that they've already failed. This means that we must make sure that whatever the diet of curriculum, it enables them to be successful. It's a balance of not offering them something that's too simple and too easy or making it so challenging that it's off the scale. It's a continuous balance, though continually assessing, then tweaking and changing. Just to watch it in action is a thing of great joy, and I'm very lucky I get to go round different hospital schools and to look at how it works for pupils.

Is there any thought nationally to professional development for colleagues who are working in this space?

That is an interesting question, because in fact, the children that we have in hospital and in our APs are mainstream children. This means that in terms of teachers' pedagogical knowledge and subject knowledge, they need access to mainstream CPD. Otherwise, if they don't keep up, then there's a risk of not offering the children what they need. Alongside the CPD, colleagues also need to understand the impact of an illness on a child's ability to take on new learning and to assimilate and remember information. This is affected by conditions such as chronic fatigue syndrome and long COVID, where children say that they have brain fog. It's about being sensitive to this because there isn't a course where we can learn about the impact of illness on a young person's learning.

What we have tried to do through the National Association for Hospital Education is to link colleagues together. We have subject networks run by peers, for peers, and if somebody messages me and they are a new head in the hospital sector, we make sure one of us mentors them, supports them, invites them for visits, and we make sure they're part of our leadership groups. We also find the SEND network helpful. We ask whether there is anyone who can share their expertise for individual cases. It's about creating something sustainable where people can access that information. It's such a joy to witness the generosity of sharing and collaboration in this sector.

By way of final words, if you have a child in your school who goes into hospital, do please link up with your hospital school, give them a ring, go in, and visit children because they do suffer from social isolation. I cannot stress enough how important it is for a child to belong to their home school. Letters from their classmates can make a real difference. If you're sending work, you could put a little note inside or send an email to let them know that they're not forgotten. This is so important because one child said that during the pandemic when lessons were online that they were living their best life: 'I'm just one of the other children in the class.'

Poor health is never an excuse

A conversation with Stephen Deadman

Stephen Deadman is the headteacher of the Children's Hospital School in Leicester.

Please could you tell us a little bit about what a hospital school is and the provision you are in charge of?

Essentially, hospital education is for any child who is missing school because of their health. We have four sites. I'm headteacher across the whole organisation. We have a head of school who runs each site. Two of those provisions are inpatient provisions within a hospital and the other two are our own schools on alternative provision sites.

The first provision is at the Leicester Royal Infirmary, which is a big general hospital in Leicester. There are nine children's wards with between 20 and 30 children every day who need educating. Some have been in for a few days, some have been in for several months. Sometimes they could be in there for up to six months. And then you've got those children who come back regularly, so they might be coming back for regular treatment, for cystic fibrosis or for chemotherapy, for example. So we would pick up those children who come back regularly straight away because we know them.

You never know who's going to be admitted. So, we have to assemble a staff team that can cover all bases. We've got a few SEN teachers who teach our PMLD students. We've got a few primary colleagues, one Early Years, and then the rest will be a mix of secondary colleagues. Between the team we provide for all the children, and colleagues have to teach out of their comfort zone. They have to be flexible.

The second hospital provision is a CAMHS psychiatric inpatient unit with 15 beds for children with complex mental health needs. Often the young people there are under section and will be there for a period of time, often at least five weeks, some for longer. The young people are mainly secondary age.

And then we have our two alternative provisions, which are our largest operations. They are for children who live at home but are too ill to go into their mainstream school. There are a few primary children but it's essentially a secondary provision, mainly for Year 10 and 11 students who have fallen out of their secondary school due to poor mental health as a result of bullying and other issues, including eating disorders. We've got some students with physical health needs, including chronic fatigue and long COVID. These pupils can't go into mainstream, so we generally would keep them with us, particularly in KS4. They come to us and we work with them to go to post-16 rather than try to get them back to their own school, because that's quite tricky for them.

Then, we've got our other provision, which is for younger children. And for those we really do try to get them back into school. Or they might come, get an EHCP, and then move to a specialist setting rather than go back to their mainstream school. The two alternative provisions are for children who are dual registered. They're all on roll with us and at mainstream schools.

Finally, the newest provision we've got, which still takes place within those two AP schools, is a short-term intervention; to qualify for a place, young people would have to be referred by a CAMHS worker or a paediatrician. The threshold to reach CAMHS is so high now, it means there's a huge number of children who are still suffering with anxiety and are beginning to miss school. Their attendance is falling, but they're just on a hugely long waiting list for CAMHS. That's why we introduced a new short-term provision for those children where they would come to us for two or three days a week for eight weeks. It's early intervention, really. If we can intervene at that point and get them back into school then, hopefully, they won't need that longer-term CAMHS referral in the future. The SEND and AP Green Paper published the three-tier model of support, where Tier 1 is outreach work in schools – we do a lot of training and support for schools and have our own CPD offer; Tier 2 is short-term interventions, which is the new provision I have just described; and Tier 3 is for those longer-term transitional placements where they might be with us for one or two years, and then we focus on them going to a specialist provision or on to a post-16 setting. We provide those three layers of support for schools and children.

Beginning with the Leicester Royal Infirmary, how do you go about structuring your curriculum for your young people?

So the children at the hospital would follow the curriculum that their main school is following because the vast majority will leave the hospital and go back to their mainstream school. Every morning our ward leader logs on to the computer and she sees which children have been admitted. Most of the children are still there. You know, we've planned the next day, anyway. But obviously, there'll be new admissions, or people that are discharged overnight. Generally, we don't pick children up until about day five and then, once we know who's in, the ward leader allocates the staff, trying to match them to the year group or the particular phase that they are specialists in.

As soon as a child's been admitted, our admin person will contact the home school and say, 'So-and-so has been admitted. Can you let us know where they're up to? What topic they're doing?' And most schools are great and will get back reasonably quickly. We ask our schools to be quite specific rather than just say, 'We're doing the Romans.' We want to know what, specifically, they are doing this week. The whole idea is that when they rejoin their class they haven't missed out on that learning. If we're not sure, or if schools don't come back to us quickly with the work, then, you know, we've got some expert primary teachers who can conduct baseline tests and they will be asked to set some English and maths work, for example. The staff are recently out of mainstream schools, so they are very skilled in knowing that this year group, at this time, should be doing this or that kind of thing.

With primary children we try to join in with the home school as much as we can. One primary school had an assembly, for example, and we could log on with the iPad at this child's bed, and they could be part of the assembly, remotely. There was also a class reading activity that the primary school were doing, and our child was sat in their bed with their iPad and could join in.

Those who are doing GCSEs or A-levels in hospital can usually log on to their school account and pick up the work from there. So, often it's more of a tutoring role; the members of staff at the home school can teach them the concepts and our staff consolidate the learning. But again, even at KS3 and KS4, our staff are good at baseline assessments and working out what the children should be studying.

What does a lesson look like in a hospital school?

You know, the lessons are magical! One lad was interested in the Titanic. So, one of our members of staff began with a D&T lesson, where the pupil made a cardboard model of the Titanic. Then they moved on to science where he learned about density and floating. Then the pupil made a video and was able to put the background on and used Lego figures to create an animation. So, just from the pupil's interest in the Titanic, they've done a bit of history, they've done a bit of D&T, a bit of science, and then they've done some film making and learned about animation and storytelling.

How far do you allow teachers that kind of autonomy when planning what they teach?

They have a great deal of autonomy. For pupils who have been in hospital for a while, when our teachers turn up at the bedside it's often the highlight of their day, because every other time someone visits, they may be prodding them or injecting them or doing things that are not very nice. So, our staff make the learning exciting and have the chance to follow pupils' interests. If they're in hospital, they should still have access to proper science and some experiments, because you don't want to disadvantage them twice, once by being in hospital and twice by serving up a lukewarm, half-baked offer. It doubly disadvantages them.

If children are able to come down, we've got a nice little classroom. We've got an Early Years corner for water and soft play, and stuff like that. And then we've got our KS2 corner and our secondary corner. So, all in one class serving all year groups.

What are the main challenges of that provision, and how do you overcome them?

The layout of the hospital means the wards aren't all together – they're on different floors. The children's heart surgery is in a different building. Our staff do lots of miles! They have to lug resources around and pay close attention to infection control.

Colleagues have to be really flexible. If you have a member of staff who says, 'I only teach KS2,' then it's not really going to work out. But our staff are wonderful; they will have a go at anything. We train our teachers so they're all comfortable doing work with those who have profound learning needs, primary and secondary.

Who you are going to teach next is not always easy to tell. Sometimes you plan to go see a child, and they're asleep, or the doctor's with them, or they're down in the physio gym, which scuppers things. You just have to adjust. You go to see someone else, and then you come back later. Staff have to be flexible in that respect too. And even within a lesson, things can change. I watched a lesson recently and the pupil just put his blanket over his head. He really wasn't feeling it, so the teacher stopped what she was doing and then it was just about seeing what might engage the pupil. So, it's not sticking rigidly to your plan. It's being flexible within that lesson as well when the health needs are not right. Sometimes, what that child needs – when they're deeply upset because they're worried or they're in pain – is someone just to talk to and to have a story read to them. It's having the emotional intelligence to recognise that. You can't just plough on with what you've planned. That's the same for any teaching, but it's heightened, because there's so much more that could be affecting the child.

Tell us about the CAMHS unit.

We have 15 residential beds. We are not always full. Some children are there on a voluntary basis, although fewer now than maybe in the past. The complexity of the mental health issues has gone up.

Again, we try to match the curriculum from their home school, but often they haven't really been engaged with education for a while prior to admission. We contact the school, and we find out where they are with their studies, and we try to continue with that work so that they can engage.

As a back-up, we have what we call 'units of work'. There are 12 units of work for English, maths, science, PSHE and art. If somebody comes in and they haven't been in school for a long time, or they don't know what they're doing or school haven't come back to us, those 12-unit schemes give us a framework that we can work through.

We've also got our 'Engagement Profile'. It's not the same as the engagement model for PMLD children. It's for those young people who are not ready to move from the residential block over to the school block and engage in the educational element of the provision. They're not well enough to engage in education just yet because their mental health is not right; for instance, some experience psychosis. So, we have engagement activities on a one-to-one basis, to build a relationship, to settle them down, to improve their social skills and to try to build some kind of trust in relationships. It could be an art project or some joint reading and poetry, or whatever; they are specific activities to engage that child who isn't yet ready for education.

They are generally with us for a long time, and they get a balance of English, maths, science, art, PSHE and afternoon enrichment. We have lessons from 10am to 11am, and then a half-hour break, and then another hour lesson, then lunch, and then the afternoon is about an hour and a half. We have an English lesson, a maths lesson and/or a science lesson. And then there are more general enrichment afternoons where we might get music tutors to work with the children. There's an outdoor area. We can do some physical activity with them.

The most complex challenge is developing a curriculum for the post-16 students because they're usually not in education, employment or training (NEET). They may have enrolled at college, but colleges don't hold the place open. They've often done GCSEs. They're not on a particular course, or don't know what they want to do next. And of course, for a lot of those young people the idea of thinking about the future, when, to some, there isn't a future, can be hugely difficult. So, a few years ago, we introduced AQA Unit Awards for those students, because there were short pieces of work that were relevant and/or achievable. And they get some sense of achievement. They get a certificate for what they've done. It could be something around food hygiene or CV writing, that kind of thing, which is pertinent and might be useful for them. They can see some purpose to doing it rather than engaging on a long academic course that they might not want to do or end up completing.

The two sites we haven't spoken about yet – your AP sites we might call them – let's move on to those.

All the students live at home. They're all dual registered with their home schools. The majority are secondary; we've got one or two primary children. That's a new provision we're just starting to grow.

Numbers have definitely increased. When I first joined the school, we might have reached 60 children by the end of the year in total across the whole school. But then last year we got to 97. For the last five years we've never gone above 35 students in Year 11; this year in Year 11 we've already got 43 and it's only November. We have two criteria: they must be too ill to attend school, and this must be supported by CAMHS or a paediatrician. There has been an increase in mental health issues; it's not just anxiety, it's quite serious, like self-harm, eating disorders and suicidal ideation. We also see a significant number with diabetes that they're not managing so well.

We do a bit of remote learning, but when a pupil is referred and they're given a place at our school, the expectation is that they attend in person. For some students that is really difficult to begin with. A typical narrative is that we go to the home and the child is in the bedroom and you talk through the door to them. We've had staff who have sat on the stairs, played the guitar, read a story, and then, after a few weeks, the child might come downstairs and meet you at the dining room table, and begin having some lessons. Fast forward six months or a year, and they're in our school, attending full-time, getting great GCSEs and going on to college. So that's the kind of journey for some students. Most can come into the school straight away, and it might only be for a couple of half days, but as soon as we build their confidence then we can start building up.

Our main building is for secondary. It's an education centre for children with mental health issues. There are some with physical needs, like chronic fatigue or bowel and eating problems. We describe it as a mini secondary school; it's got a science lab, a drama room, a kitchen, a dining room – all the rooms that you would get in a secondary school. It's just smaller and quieter. We want them to enjoy school again, and love being back at school, and they do. They say that they love it. It's quiet. The teaching and learning is excellent. We've made a point of making sure our lessons are as good as you would get in the very best mainstream schools.

If we think about Years 10 and 11, the majority of them have been out of mainstream education for six months to a year. They have not been in any kind of education, and even when they were, it was very part-time, or they were going to a quiet room at the front of school. So they've been out of education for a long, long time. When they leave at the end of their time with us, we want them to be ready for further study, which means three things: getting good academic grades; being ready for work; and being ready for life. So, we design and deliver our own curriculum. They've all come from different schools, and you can't teach 20 different specifications for different subjects. They've also been out of school for so long. Often you're trying to deliver, say, maths GCSE in a year on a part-time timetable, with the students having missed a chunk of school. It's a big ask of our staff to teach a full GCSE in less time with sporadic student attendance. They can do maths, English language and literature, double or triple science, and then they can do two options from film studies, health and social care or art. Students who attend well can finish with seven or eight GCSEs. Our students regularly get loads of grade 8s and grade 9s. If they are able and they attend, we provide the environment, small classes and the brilliant teaching that can get them to achieve at the highest level.

Beyond the subjects I've just described, they have a PSHE lesson, a PE lesson, relationships and sex education lesson, and computing. And then we have a personal development slot where they will do things like Duke of Edinburgh, personal finance or citizenship.

So that's our traditional curriculum, and then layered on top of that is all the therapeutic stuff. So, children might come out of lessons for art therapy or music, or they might do some cooking in small groups.

We use the school-led tutoring funding for extra tuition in English, maths and science, and then also for film, art, and health and social care. You use those interventions to help students do the controlled assessments by the board deadlines. We also provide reading interventions.

It's a very comprehensive package that we offer; the more they attend, the more of that they can tap into, and you might have some students only there for one or two days a week, or arrive very late in Year 11, and they might just do English and maths or English, maths and science, or some would just do functional skills because they've just been out of education for so long.

In terms of personal support, our lead pastoral manager delivers Thrive. We baseline the children academically, and then put them on a particular pathway. Similarly, our Thrive baselines their individual personal developmental needs. Before that the therapeutic offer was a bit hit and miss. We sort of tried stuff out. But with Thrive we're being more directive. Each child completes the initial assessment and then we say, 'Right, this pupil needs this kind of intervention, or this one. They, on the other hand, might benefit from reading a certain author, or listening to this music, or equine therapy.' Sometimes we go in and do things in the same way, though we plan our taught curriculum based on some baselining. We try to do that with the therapeutic side as well. So it's a bit more targeted rather than a bit more scattergun, as it may have been in the past.

What about the other AP provision?

That's for our longer-term KS3 pupils. Curriculum provision is very similar: English, maths, science, French, humanities – almost all the national curriculum subjects.

These children are with CAMHS, and they're with us for a long period of time, one or two years, but with the younger ones. That's because it's a separate building. We're really trying to focus on transition, either back to their home school or back to a different mainstream school, or some will get an EHCP while they're with us, and then they might go to a special school. Occasionally they might remain with us and move to the Year 10 and 11 provision. But we try to get the younger children back into their community, really, because although we're a Leicester school, we take children from Leicester, Leicestershire and Rutland as well. Some children might come from Melton, Loughborough, Hinckley, etc., which is up to an hour in a taxi, so the more who can go back and remain in their community, even if it's a bit tough to begin with, is, we think, on the whole, the best outcome. It is difficult to get them back. It's not easy if you've been in a school that is causing you anxiety, or you've been bullied, and now you're at a place where you love to be, and you get up in the morning and parents are seeing a happy child.

And then the other part of that provision is the short-term places. It operates a bit like a traditional alternative provision. A mainstream headteacher will commission a place here for so many weeks. We've got two groups of pupils. There's a two-day-a-week group, and there's a three-day-a-week group and they attend between six and eight weeks. After week four, there's a review meeting and, to be honest, almost everybody's stay is extended to eight weeks. And the feedback we've had from schools is that eight weeks isn't quite enough, so from the summer term 2024 we're going to extend it to 12.

In the last few weeks, we came up with a transition plan back to school. We've got an inclusion worker who goes to the school and meets the staff. The member of staff comes to see us, sits with the child, sees what they've been doing, that they've attended, they can engage, and they notice the difference. And then we work with the home school to come up with a transition plan. Who's the key member of staff? Who's going to meet them on the gate? We are very detailed. For some children it's worked brilliantly; when they came to us, they hadn't been in school for months and now they're back in full-time. For some though, it's slow, or it's okay to begin with, and then it drops off a bit, and then you get schools asking if they can refer again. And so that's not ideal. Where's the end point? So maybe 12 weeks might be what is needed.

The two-day-a-week provision is largely for Years 5, 6 and 7. That is less academic and more about nurturing them. They do English and maths. The three-day-a-week group is for Years 8, 9 and 10 and there's a stronger focus on the academic – English, maths, science and PE. The focus is still on building the social skills, building resilience, getting them to think about going back to school.

Tell us about how you have developed your CPD offer.

Since COVID, our numbers have risen dramatically. We reached a point where we were physically full, and we had to do something different. So we began saying to schools, 'Can one of our members of staff come into your school and see what's going on?' It really just started out of necessity and the fact that we had a waiting list. The child who was in school would be desperate for some help, so we just sent a member of staff in for an afternoon to try to see what was going on and come up with a plan to help, and schools said that's really useful. It's this whole idea of catching children upstream before it gets too much; a kind of early intervention plan.

This is a three-tier approach. Tier one is outreach work in schools. We have a member of staff who is accredited to deliver the two-day mental health first aid course. She can also deliver a one-day mental health champion course, and then a half-day mental health awareness course. And we've started putting on hour-long virtual training, about supporting children with eating disorders, self-harm, neurodiversity and anxiety as well as trauma attachment. They are hour-long Zoom CPD sessions, and some schools and trusts are asking us to deliver those face-to-face to groups of staff, after school or on an INSET day. Working with a local sixth form college we're now piloting training for their young people in the sixth form to help them support each other. It's also suitable for parents.

Ultimately, the driving force behind everything we do is to be aspirational for the children, and not use poor health as an excuse for not providing the very best teaching. When I arrived, we were a 'good' school; we have since had two 'outstanding' inspections and we've transformed our provision. We understand that there are health needs – we manage that – but our priority is to provide the best curriculum we can. We want to be ambitious; we want them to have access to the best teaching and learning in a really supportive caring environment. We get ex-students coming back, having finished university. That's incredibly satisfying.

The importance of the arts and wider opportunities

A conversation with Sarah Marrion

Sarah Marrion is a deputy headteacher at Wirral Hospitals' School, Joseph Paxton Campus

First of all, can you tell us how you got into the world of alternative provision?

I had been a musician for a number of years, then went into voluntary work, and then decided to become a teacher. After about 17 years in mainstream – where I had a number of roles including teaching performing arts – I then became a director of business enterprise while I was working in a specialist school. I then became an assistant head in charge of teaching and learning with responsibility for music in a hospital school. We have approximately 80 pupils aged between 11 and 16 and they join us having gone through an admissions panel. We're a hospital in the sense that the young person comes to us with a medical diagnosis and their admission is supported by a specialist medical professional who has declared that the young person is too unwell to attend a mainstream setting.

I have been there about nine years and have found music to make a difference to young people who joined the school with a diagnosis of very poor mental health, often comorbid with neurodiversity. What I had in front of me were lots of people with amazing skills and talents that had just been silenced through their time in mainstream and through their illnesses and/or neurodiversity.

We expanded the music and developed a performing arts curriculum together with a programme called Learning for Life. As a school we focus on building resilience to help with transition back into mainstream education. For many of our students, they don't join us until they are in KS4, so their transition is into mainstream post-16 education.

What's extraordinary about your curriculum?

What's extraordinary about our curriculum is that we manage to match the academic progress while ensuring that every aspect of our school, from our environment to our teaching methods, supports our students' mental health issues. So we start every day by asking, 'What does that young person need? What does it look like?' In terms of our delivery, we offer a very full and varied curriculum. We have a routine timetable, but each child's day within this timetable will be slightly bespoke based on their health needs. A child comes to us and does all of the national curriculum subjects at KS3, and they can leave us with up to eight GCSEs at grade 5 and above, or they might leave us with four or five GCSEs or Level 1 qualifications. Our curriculum is broad enough for students to go on to study A-levels.

A few years ago, I applied for funding from the Arts Council. We decided to work with the Open Eye Gallery, and through the project we found that pupils were able to use the camera as a tool to 'hide behind' in a similar way to our music students using an instrument to speak for them or our drama students creating a new self to speak through, then becoming more confident in getting out and exploring. What started as an experimental project has resulted in having photography on our curriculum and becoming one of our most popular and successful GCSE options courses.

We have always previously offered music at GCSE and now offer a Performing Arts Vocational Award, which allows our students to opt for music, drama, make-up and sound technician specialisms. This is a relatively new course, both to our school and to the suite of options available from the exam boards. It is still in its infancy here, but our students value the fact that they can choose a discipline within this course that suits their skills and special interests.

Can you tell us more about the music curriculum?

We use music as a therapeutic tool to get young people playing together. We have a significant number of young people who have selective mutism. So, the question is how can we support them to work with one another in the classroom?

We have found that they can communicate with their instruments. We will model communication by saying, for example, 'Should we try this chord?' or 'Should we try this piece of music?' And then we can step back as teachers and the children are communicating with each other through the instruments. We step away completely, and they start playing together, and then actually start speaking to each other.

There are many different aspects for performing arts and we find that there's a role for everyone. For example, one young person was very nervous and found it hard to socialise. We have an old-fashioned proscenium arch stage, and with support from a teaching assistant, this student in Year 8 was responsible for opening and closing the curtains. The next year he worked on the spotlights out in the auditorium, mixing, not just hidden behind the curtains. And then, finally, he was on the lighting desk, which meant he had to work with other students. He's got to design. He's got to communicate. And he's working now in a much bigger group of people and is a central part of the crew. The focus is about building a young person's resilience and self-worth. We are fortunate in that we've got the time to do that. We find that if young people feel successful, they are ready to learn and that means that they also achieve well academically.

We also have an annual Enterprise Week. The students work in teams across year groups. The main focus is on 'Fundraise for a Fiver'. We give pupils £5 notes, and they're told that this is a loan and they've got to make a profit. Pupils work in teams across year groups. This helps them to communicate and to learn from pupils outside their normal class or year group.

They have five days to create their business idea, which finishes with a marketplace.

We invite parents, visitors and local business people throughout the week. Year 11 students are given roles as directors, which means they can include their leadership and work skills on their CVs.

Last year we turned the school into a holiday resort – 'Costa del Paxton' – because our site is the Joseph Paxton Campus. There was an entertainment group, a spa and an animal hotel! The pupils also created their own currency. We also had a front-of-house team desk, and pupils could book onto the different activities throughout the week. There was also a business network lunch, which meant that the catering students had to work to a budget and consider dietary requirements. What we are doing is using the curriculum to develop confidence and resilience. Many of our young people and their families feel invisible, and we want them to be fully functioning, participating members of society. We want them to be able to have employment. Our school motto is 'Working together to make everything better'.

Do you have any students who join you and then go back into mainstream?

It can be very difficult to help students make the transition back to mainstream, due both to their illnesses and their experiences of being in that environment. The majority of pupils don't join us until the end of Year 9 or later. Therefore, most of these pupils tend to stay with us, and our year groups will double in number between Year 9 and Year 11, which means we have to be careful that we are not too full at KS3 to allow for the increase in numbers further up the school. At the end of KS4, all pupils need to be ready to go to one of the local colleges, and we take care to work closely with them and with pupils' families by creating individual, transitional learning plans.

Can you tell us about the Learning for Life programme?

The Learning for Life programme incorporates PSHE, culture, diversity, careers education and citizenship. The students have one lesson with a classroom teacher and one lesson with our learning mentors. Through joint planning we are able to deliver the practical and creative elements of this curriculum that also help to build our students' cultural capital.

For example, if we are teaching about finance, our mentors will go out with young people to a shop and handle money and different forms of payment. We can then also incorporate the development of other skills such as road safety, communicating in the real world and personal care.

As part of preparation for adulthood, we also make a point of sitting down together around a dining room table and eating together. Some young people don't like eating in front of others, so we provide these experiences in a low-risk way.

Also, as part of our broader Learning for Life programme, we offer a wide variety of interventions and sensory breaks that help young people learn how to self-regulate and prepare for learning. These include things like gardening, boxing, sensory games, music, etc.

Our school shows that a low arousal environment and setting, without the pressure of uniform and homework, can provide the conditions for our pupils to gain qualifications and thrive. The most important thing we do for our pupils is celebrate their individuality: by doing this we help them to get ready to learn and experience the joy of life again.

High academic aspirations for *all* pupils

A conversation with Martin Gray

Martin Gray is assistant headteacher with responsibility for teaching, learning and the curriculum at Newcastle Bridges School.

Please tell us about your background.

I have been a teacher for 27 years. The first 18 were in mainstream education in the Northeast teaching English, and I also had middle leadership responsibilities. Then I moved to be English coordinator at Newcastle Bridges where I am an assistant head. Newcastle Bridges School is a school that meets a huge variety of complex pupil needs. My role now is to look after curriculum as well as teaching and learning. We are a multi-site organisation in Newcastle and Northumberland with a shared designation for educating pupils in hospital, including a secure mental health facility and alternative provision. We have teaching teams based in each of the locations, and the pupils we teach can be either long term or short term and from Early Years to age 19.

Let's take your main hospital school – could you tell us about what kind of needs pupils have there? And what kind of curriculum provision you start to shape with your team there?

We have learners with PMLD through to students with anorexia or bulimia, for example, who are very high attainers. This means that we need to meet the needs across the spectrum. Our teachers are very adept and are trained to deliver to pupils across ages and differing prior attainment. We have staff who are experienced in delivering to pupils with PMLD and others able to deliver at GCSE and A-level. To make this work, specialists might work across more than one site, as I do for English. This requires great flexibility as some pupils might only be with us for a short term and others for longer stays.

So, this means you could have a 17-year-old with anorexia, and they are taking A-levels in psychology, sociology, music and English. How do you support that student?

We have some flexibility and can employ people from outside. We have a team of staff who work on a more ad hoc basis, who have expertise in delivering subjects at a high level. We also work closely with the students' home schools as they provide work for us. This means we can deliver that work and facilitate the students in terms of the learning they need to do. COVID meant that colleagues became adept at remote learning. This means that our staff can support learners with the curriculum being delivered from their home school. We work to get the students the best deal possible, based on the resources we have available to us.

What we find is that our students are very motivated. Their experiences in hospital are often difficult, so the idea of escaping into education for a few hours a day is very appealing to them. Often, we are teaching at the bedside while medical procedures are going on around us. It's very humbling.

When we were inspected, we made sure that the inspection team saw every aspect of the school. I don't think they were prepared for what they saw. For example, there was a girl having a science lesson at the bedside when the inspector arrived, and afterwards her father spoke to him to say that his daughter had received so much support from the team. 'They are sent from God!'

It is very humbling to listen to you talking about how keen your students are to engage in education. What is also striking is the wide range of expertise and flexibility from you and your colleagues.

We need to think carefully about how we are deploying staff and how we're utilising all the resources available to us, given the range of students' needs. We also put a significant focus on relationships so that we build trust, particularly for those who have been reluctant to attend mainstream school. We find that these students, many in our alternative provision, will come into lessons if we have first established trust with them. Often, they have not had good experiences in the past, and seeing their attendance rise is one of the indicators that we are doing a good job. This year, just over half of the 20+ Year 11 students in our AP study GCSE maths, English and science, and some will take functional skills or entry-level qualifications – 90% of students left with a grade 4 or above in GCSE English language and about 89% in GCSE biology. These results are achieved through the support of teachers and teaching assistants who are very skilled at supporting our students with gaps in their learning.

We are responsive to the needs and prior attainment of students. For example, some students take a foundation science GCSE at the end of Year 10, and a recent cohort were particularly keen, so they embarked on biology, physics and chemistry. It meant that students in an AP were able to leave with triple science. I think that is quite remarkable, really. We did this by having drop-down sessions in addition to their regular lessons. We had students who achieved grade 8s and 9s in GCSE English language and GCSE art last year.

Is it a priority to get KS3 students back into mainstream?

We have two transition classes. Some of the students are referred to us from the local authority through a local inclusion panel and a triage system. This involves a meeting every fortnight to decide which would be the best provision for individual students. They might be referred to us on a six- or 12-week placement. We have a KS3 class and a KS4 class for the rolling programme. We generally have two students joining us each week either for KS3 or KS4. For KS3 the provision is along the lines of a primary model with a class teacher who delivers the core to them, and then they join our main school for the more extended curriculum, such as music, PE, humanities and design and technology, which are delivered by specialists.

The KS4 group will have a more diverse range of teachers. Our first cohort of placement students are due to return to mainstream at the end of the term. In addition, we have a cohort of students who've been with us for a long time, some of them since Year 7, who are now in Year 10 and Year 11, and we have looked after their education throughout.

What is special about your KS3 curriculum? Is there anything noteworthy that we wouldn't expect to find elsewhere?

We have been involved in a forest school project with Newcastle University for about nine years. It was designed to support engagement and mental health. On Friday, students in Years 7 and 8 work at the Forest School, and we find it is very rewarding for them. On Wednesday afternoons the timetable is collapsed, and students have a choice of different enrichment activities within or outside school. This might be art, crafts or music, for example. We also have traditional sports activities such as playing football and visits to an indoor climbing wall. Some students visit a riding stable where they can learn to ride and about stable management. Some might go to Kirkley Hall, an agricultural college, where they learn about small animal care. Students find these activities very rewarding and attendance on a Wednesday is always very high!

How would you respond to anyone who pressed you and said that these children have had a poor academic experience in school, and they get even less academic work when they come to you? I'm only being provocative.

They still get five lessons of English, maths and science, together with lessons in humanities, music, computing and everything else considered part of a broad KS3 curriculum. I think you'll find with us that students are attending 80–90% of the time, whereas in mainstream they wouldn't have been. They're accessing more lessons in addition to the extracurricular opportunities and there's significant buy-in from students due to this balance.

When we interviewed John d'Abbro, who runs a series of facilities in East London, he came out with a stunning phrase that the mainstream isn't good enough for these children. That's not a blame game. Yours and similar settings have the capacity to offer bespoke provision in small classes, which means students can get the attention and support they need.

I'd agree with John's comment, but we operate with small groups and can make our provisions more bespoke. We treat our young people as individuals with very disparate needs. For example, a student who might not have slept well the night before might need an additional break or snack so that we can make that a successful day for them.

What destinations do your students have? You say that some of them are integrated back into the school system. Presumably there's some outreach and negotiation with the host school?

Some students return to their 'home' school and go into the sixth form. Some go to local colleges and continue their studies there. We have good links with providers and put in significant support for transition because we recognise that this can be a huge step for them.

To turn to the hospital provision, I am interested in what it looks like for primary students.

There is support from the home school and we have to remember that very often these pupils are quite unwell. We have two specialist staff with backgrounds in KS1, and we focus on developing the core skills and putting smiles on their faces! We aim to provide a level of normality, and it's wonderful to see them having success in their learning in spite of what they have been through.

How important is consistency of staff? Do you have problems with staff turnover?

Many of our staff have been with us for a long time. This means they can build long-term relationships with both students and colleagues in all the agencies we work with. We work hard to keep staff and retrain them where necessary. For example, our nursery manager went on to complete a degree, supported by us, and has stayed with the organisation, having started as a learning support assistant. We also have colleagues who have completed teacher apprenticeships and are both now working within the provision. Once we identify good staff, we work hard to keep them.

As part of our ongoing professional learning, we work with the local Education Psychology Service and with Kalmer Counselling on trauma-informed practice. CPD is very bespoke, so that we are in the best position to support our students.

Bridging the gap between AP and mainstream

A conversation with Gemma Blacow

Gemma Blacow is assistant principal at CP Riverside School in Nottingham.

I was a mainstream English teacher for about 12 years and the trust gave me an opportunity to go on secondment to an alternative provision setting as an assistant principal in charge of curriculum. I'm now in my fourth year and absolutely love working in alternative provision. I work at CP Riverside, a free school for up to 51 students within the East Midlands Education trust in Nottingham.

CP Riverside aims to provide a curriculum that bridges the gap between what would normally be considered a typical AP and mainstream. This means we give students a diet that allows our students to compete with their peers. Alongside this, we include relational teaching, coaching and other opportunities that they wouldn't necessarily get in mainstream.

We have a phased entry for students joining CP Riverside. Once students have been referred to us, they come to look around and meet the staff. It's a chance for us to find out a bit about them and why they need alternative provision. It's important to listen to them and find out how they feel, because it can be quite daunting for them. Then they join us for a two-day induction to trial some lessons. They meet a number of staff including the principal who walks through the way the school works and the ambition the school has for its students. This is followed by a six-week trial, and if that goes well, they enrol full-time unless they need a phased introduction, possibly with support from their home school, when a teaching assistant might support them at the beginning.

Our hope is that the students will go on the journey with us and that they will integrate into our school, and we take them through to Year 11 and get them ready for post-16, and the world of work and life. It's not just about building them up in terms of the grades they need for the next step. It's also about building them up as a whole person. Many students are lacking confidence, so we support them with that as well as with their grades.

When I started here, I thought that the curriculum would be limited, and I was surprised to find that the students who came in were entitled to the same academic diet as any young person in a mainstream school. It was far more than functional skills and a few vocational courses. In fact, our students take English language and literature, maths and science along with a choice of academic and vocational pathway subjects.

Can you tell us how you develop students' confidence and wellbeing?

I found that in my last role as head of year I had 238 students to look after, and it was hard to know every one of them. By contrast, at CP Riverside we know every student inside out. We know their foibles. We know the things they like; we know what makes them tick. We believe that coaching can make a difference to students and adults, so everyone has a coach. This supports our work on developing relationships and working on restorative practice. We check in with our coachees every morning and at the end of each day.

In the mornings, the students will journal either by writing down how they are feeling or by talking to us. We see this as checking their 'climate' each day. How are they doing? Is their day going to go as they think? Or do we need to change it around a bit? One of the things I love about my work is that we can change the timetable to make it work for students that day. We have a sensory room and connection rooms where they can talk to someone. Then, just as importantly, we do this at the end of the day to see how their day has gone.

Once a week we have 'connection' time at the end of the day where we support students' emotional literacy, resilience and ability to communicate. On another day, again at the end of the school day, we work in small groups to connect to 'place'. It might be a film club or sports. We do a lot of sport because of the benefits of playing together and developing team spirit. We aim to give our students plenty of experiences, such as going to cafés and trips to London, organised by the memorable experiences team.

Memorable experiences are built into the daily routines: for the first 45 minutes of the day, we have memorable experiences and activities. It might be board games or talking, painting or going to the park. Students in KS3 have taken the 'Bikeability' cycle training, and they have also built a bike from scratch! It is possible to support students' confidence over time. For example, we had one young person who would not leave the office when he joined us, but who recently went to London and was able to go on the Tube. We have also been able to support his interest in music production and it's meant he has been able to collaborate with another student on their joint project. We believe that when they go on to post-16 they should be level with their peers and should be entitled to the same experiences as other students. Our KS4 curriculum seeks to ensure that students spend as much time as possible learning in areas that are of interest and relevance for them now and in the future. KS4 students benefit from enrichment being intertwined with careers and pathway curriculum choices. There will be a greater emphasis on core and pathway subjects working together. Students choose one pathway subject in Year 10 and then a complementing one in Year 11 that is taught by the same staff member.

In terms of ongoing professional development for staff, we have a weekly teaching and learning briefing. The fact that we are part of a trust means that we are able to draw on the subject expertise of colleagues.

AP Huh

If there's one thing that particularly stands out for you about CP Riverside, what would it be?

The staff, because every single one of them is invested in the school. There's no one fighting against it. Everyone's there because they know it's a good place to be and a good place to work, and every single colleague champions every student. We find that visitors comment on the great environment for our young people and that's exactly what we want to create for them: a safe and stimulating place for them to learn.

What advice would you give to mainstream colleagues about alternative provision?

If you can, go and visit an AP. I collaborate with mainstream staff for visits to CP Riverside. This is important because we've got to blur the line between the mainstream and AP. And we can do that by forging relationships. This is where being in a trust is helpful because staff come to us and vice versa. We can learn a lot from each other.

Lessons from AP into mainstream

A conversation with Sarah Jones

Sarah Jones is vice principal in a mainstream secondary school.

It's a pleasure to have you here, Sarah. Could you begin by telling us how you got into the world of alternative provision?

I was a head in a small mainstream school and saw a job advertised for an executive vice principal across four alternative provision settings with the Wellspring Trust in Lincolnshire, with pupils aged from four to 16. I then moved to Buckinghamshire where I was executive head of an alternative provision. I've now moved back into mainstream as a vice principal. I have responsibility for inclusion and behaviour, and I am trying to bring what I've learned in AP back into mainstream. I am aiming to have an impact a bit further upriver and to stop pupils falling into the river, so to speak.

Can you tell us about what alternative provision looks like in Early Years and KS1?

It breaks your heart that there are children so young who have been permanently excluded from school. We had children in Year 1 and occasionally in reception whose behaviour was so extreme that their school had applied for a placement. If a child that young is not able to be in a mainstream it is usually due to the horrific things that had happened to them which meant that their behaviour was not manageable in a mainstream classroom. While many had tragic stories, the beautiful thing about working in an AP setting is that you have the chance to build provision that meets their needs.

When I started, we had mixed-age primary classrooms, with lower primary for reception and Years 1 and 2, and upper primary for pupils in Years 3 to 5.

The school's philosophy was that the curriculum should be developmental, not chronological. It meant that when we looked at a child we didn't say, 'You are in Year 7, therefore you should study XYZ.' Instead, we asked where they were developmentally and what the next thing they needed was.

We found that younger pupils in lower primary were developmentally working in the Early Years Foundation Stage. For example, they were still working at shapes, and they still needed to play and to measure, and they desperately needed movement; they needed rhythm and song and to have a play basket full of costumes. They needed these formative Early Years experiences.

This meant that we were able to think creatively about their needs and to get on with that. Instead of the formal KS1 curriculum, we said that pupils in Years 2 and 3 should have free-flow access – for example, playing in a sandbox along with all the other experiences from Early Years. Our pupils deserved that kind of approach. We believe it's important for pupils, particularly those who have experienced trauma, to have access to early developmental rhythmic experiences, such as song and music and rocking, advocated by experts like psychiatrist Bruce Perry. His work has shown that such experiences are not just an important development stage for young people but also an important tool for children who've experienced trauma to go back and repair. And if you provide a free-flow play space, it means pupils can dip into things when they are ready.

For example, if a child looks as though their behaviour is escalating, we can invite them to a soft seating space and read a story together. It might be something like *We're Going on a Bear Hunt*, which has rhythm and repetition and there's a kind of comfort in it. There is a therapeutic aspect to it, because when you get it right, you can blend both the learning and the healing. It means that we're doing early language development activities with books, and we are offering a kind of closeness by sitting together on the sofa.

In alternative provision we have a fluid cohort with pupils joining and leaving us at different stages. They might have a placement and ideally we get them to a stage where they can return to mainstream. Then there are times when we have a group of children who are all at the same point. They might all be pre-phonics in that they're not ready to start shaping letters. They need to be looking at picture books, wordless books, and hearing stories, and absorbing language in that way. Other groups of pupils might be ready to learn blending sounds or going beyond CVC (consonant, vowel, consonant) words, for example. It's the benefit of AP that we have the flexibility to meet the range of needs.

You talk about continuous provision where you are providing the space, the resources, the pedagogy and the curriculum to fill some of those gaps of what children might have missed. Can you tell us about the impact of working in this way?

I obtained a grant from the Fair Education Alliance, which meant I could research how best to support pupils in early primary phases in AP. I couldn't find any other provider who had used an EYFS provision across the key stages in a PRU, and the grant enabled us to run a trial to collect and analyse data for pupils over several years. For example, we had one child whose major problem in mainstream was biting. We know that biting is often connected to an inability to express oneself and an inability to say what is needed. The child was in Year 3 and had been working through a mainstream reading curriculum, but he had patchy early reading knowledge.

He had been with us for some time before we trialled an EYFS curriculum. To begin with, the expectation had been that he needed to follow a formal curriculum. We had been logging the incidents of biting and we found that once the Early Years provision was in place, the incidents of biting went down almost overnight. It reminds me of the saying that if a flower doesn't bloom, you don't blame the flower – you fix the environment. And I thought what a phenomenal, real-life example of this little boy who had not bloomed and overnight had managed to not feel the need to bite anyone who was working with him. We ran an eight-week reading programme with him and found significant progress in his reading in terms of knowing all his sounds, starting to blend in a logical, systematic way. It was gorgeous progress on several fronts: socially, emotionally and academically.

Did you have a hunch that continuous provision was likely to be the key?

Dave Whitaker from the Wellspring Trust together with Phil Willott (who was my line manager at the time) were both committed to the model of a developmental rather than chronological curriculum. The first work I did on the curriculum was for KS4, and I had been working out how to support pupils to achieve qualifications and at the same time how to create a developmental curriculum.

At the time we had a conker tree in the playground, and there was a month every year when there were conkers everywhere. I had only been working there for a couple of months and the teenagers in the setting were fighting each other with the conkers, putting them into their pants and coming into lessons. There were conkers everywhere. I was confiscating them but they kept coming! Every moment of my life felt as though it was about conkers... I went home and was complaining to my partner about all this. He happens to be a therapist and his question was 'What are they trying to tell you, these 15-year-old boys with their conkers?', and I was like, 'Whoa! That they're horrible and they're annoying!' And he repeated, 'What are they trying to tell you, Sarah?' We got to the point where I said, 'Oh, I think they just want to play.'

I went in the next day, and we took them to a local playground. We said they could just play. And we found that these 15-year-old teenagers – usually grumpy and surly – just got on the roundabout, and pushed each other on the swings. I saw them as toddlers. I saw the little soft boys that they were inside who were enabled to move to a different space through the beauty of play. When we returned to school, the teachers in their afternoon lessons could not believe the amount of work they got through. And it made me think, 'Why on earth are we not having more play with our pupils in the primary phase?'

As it happened, when I was first appointed head of the all-through school, I had done reading and research about early learning and primary provision, because my own background had been secondary, and I knew very little about the other phases. And it was through this that I came to appreciate the importance of play. This combined with the wisdom of Dave and Phil, along with some annoying pupils and their conkers, helped to shape the provision!

I'm so glad I asked you that question. That was not what I was expecting! We've got to reclaim play as a legitimate learning process in the sector. It's not mucking about. It's not fiddling around. It is a child's deep work, isn't it? As Maria Montessori said, 'Play is the work of the child.' It would be good to know how you are bringing those principles into your current mainstream role.

As vice principal with responsibility for inclusion and pastoral in a large secondary mainstream school, having had the experience in alternative provision where you sometimes ask yourself 'why didn't someone do something sooner for some of these pupils?', the answer to my question was that maybe I should be doing that in mainstream.

I am currently working for another brilliant headteacher who lets me do all sorts of weird creative things, if I think they might work. And that's sort of the spirit of AP. We ask ourselves, 'What does this young person need?' We have an increasing cohort of pupils with emotional-based school avoidance, who either cannot get across the threshold or cannot get into lessons once they're in the building. We have young people who display that in anxious ways. We've got pupils for whom that leads to self-harm or eating disorders. And we've got pupils for whom that leads to some violent behaviour towards others.

One example of thinking laterally is working with one pupil with severe attachment difficulties who found it difficult to leave their parents. They were in Year 8 at the time, with scenes in reception when they were dropped off for school. So, we asked ourselves, 'Why can't the parent just work in my office?' We had three weeks where the parent just worked online from my office, and if their child needed them, they came into my office. Sometimes they needed to come in and speak to their parent, and sometimes the pupil could just see that they were there.

Sometimes just being in the building and knowing that their parent was also in the building was incredibly helpful for them. After about three or four weeks, the pupil was feeling more settled, so the parent moved into the car park. They would come in at the start of the day, and then go to the car park, and work from the car! True dedication from this wonderful parent!

After a couple more weeks they moved to a coffee shop in the village, and we found the slow acclimatisation – along with some access to counselling and working with CAMHS and building relationships with staff – means that the pupil now comes in every day. Their attendance is now above 97%, and if you met them now, you wouldn't know that this was a pupil who had been out of school for four months and then weeping in reception for months.

It sounds really simple, doesn't it? We'll just let the parent stay. But it's also a kind of weird thing to have a parent virtually working from the back of your office.

That's a classic case of reasonable adjustments to the power of 10. But it's also about the imagination and the humanity of you as an individual, your colleagues around you, and the institution as well. And an amazing parent too.

Our headteacher just says, 'What do you think they need?' And I say, 'I think they need this.' It means we have pupils who are on really weird packages, which I don't think would have happened when I was previously in mainstream. We have pupils who might come in just for the few lessons where they feel safe and secure with the teacher. Then they have part of their week where they work online with a tutor and part of their week where they're in school. One of them goes to a llama farm in the afternoons. In AP that kind of thing is totally normal. We have some pupils doing maths and English and some mechanics. Why is it not as normal in mainstream? With the number of pupils that we're getting who are struggling to come in, it's lovely to work for someone who just says, 'Yes, what do they need? Just do it.'

People will need to follow your example and be much more flexible and imaginative. Otherwise, we're heading for a complete disaster in terms of the number of children that are struggling in mainstream. What would you say to colleagues who are thinking 'how would I make that work in my school?' What would be the key message you'd give them?

I think if they're asking that, they are already part way there to making reasonable adjustments. Sometimes, doing things that are a bit weird can be an absolute nightmare, and sometimes it's just the most beautiful thing that you can imagine. And why not give it a shot? And I think the way that things are at the moment, there's so much that isn't working in schools for many pupils that we might ask, 'What have we got to lose? What's the worst that can happen?'

There was a London head I heard speak who said that as educators we get to build a world in our schools, which is the way that we think the world should be. That has stayed with me for my whole career. We have some power to shape and to make schools more inclusive, more welcoming, fairer and more loving and kind.

This is all carefully thought through, and it's coming from the heart as well as the intellect, and that's what's so powerful about it.

Sport was my saviour

A conversation with Eugene Dwaah

Eugene Dwaah is the CEO of the Evolution Sports Group.

Please could you tell us how you became an educator?

I became an educator through an unusual route. If you were to tell my school teachers that I ended up being a teacher, they would burst out laughing! I am probably the most unlikely individual to go back to work in a school, let alone end up being an educator.

In my youth my real interest was always sport. I played sport at an elite level. As a youngster, I was fortunate to have fantastic role models: my PE teachers, Mr Mihill and Mr Lowe. It was a real passion for them, in the old-school sense. They took me to my first trial. They took me to training at pro clubs and my county and district trials. They were exceptional in terms of their support for me in my sporting endeavours. Then I had some fantastic youth coaches. The club that I first played for was called Prince's Park, and it was run by the Metropolitan Police. The majority of coaches were police officers. The dedication they showed towards me stood me in good stead for my whole life.

My educational career really came through working for a professional football club. It was my enjoyment of coaching and being able to express myself and show others the skills I had that resonated with young people.

My mother was a teacher. My two sisters were teachers. So, I thought I'd work in a school. I found out I really enjoyed teaching. Then I went into a pastoral role, and that's where I found my calling.

I really enjoyed the pastoral work, getting to know the families, getting to know the young people, understanding what makes them tick, looking at the barriers to their learning. It resonated with me because in my teenage years I had a traumatic experience. My mother passed away when I was 15, just before I did my O levels. Sport was my saviour. My teachers were my saviours. So, that kind of pastoral work resonates with me very, very strongly.

Tell us a little bit about what happened in your first move away from football and into being your own boss.

Well, I have three kids. I was working in professional football. I really loved it. I was doing a lot of travelling, scouting players. But when the kids came along, I struggled to leave them. Sometimes I'd be on call 24/7, and I'd have to travel to Italy or Spain to look at a young player that we may have wished to sign.

So, I wanted to spend more time with the kids, to be honest. I was looking for a career that would allow me to have the school holidays with the kids, and teaching was the obvious route. And I also wanted to see why my mum, in particular, loved teaching. So, I started on that pathway, and my first job was a school in special measures. You learn a lot starting in the toughest part of London in a school that's struggling with systems and structures. And I learned so much from fantastic colleagues who were dedicated with a real passion for helping those young people – young people who have major barriers to achievement.

My first home visit really opened my eyes. I used to put a lot of pressure on a young person to do their homework, give them detentions, etc. One day I was given the opportunity to do a home visit, and when I did, it made me realise the fact that a young person was actually *in school* is a major, major success, and that they don't all have the facilities to do their homework at home. So, I started to do after-school clubs for those young people where it was overcrowded at home, or if they had some kind of illness which meant they couldn't do their homework. It made me realise I could make more of a difference if I knew more about the young people. And so that led me into the pastoral side of teaching.

What made you leave that school and set up on your own?

I was lucky. An opportunity arose to purchase, with one of my best friends, our own sports centre in a socially deprived area in Brent.

It was fantastic in terms of activities to keep the youngsters occupied during the evenings; it was the shortage of activities going on during the day time that was a problem. We had purpose-built classrooms, a lovely sports hall and a food facility. So, I approached the local authority, gave them my background and said, 'Look, I would like to start some kind of programme looking at young people at risk of falling out of school, or at risk of disengagement.' We started with a small programme and eventually became successful, particularly with our post-16 provision.

I hadn't started my company then, because I was working for a charity at the time. And then something said to me, 'Look, you know, if you really want to have some control over what you want to do in your future, you need to take the risk and go independent.' And I suspect lots of people reading this will think that the day you say 'I'm going to go on my own' is one of the scariest moments in anyone's career! But you've got to bet on yourself.

The thing is, I went into a field that I'm passionate about. And I think that's really important. I felt I was good at it. It was an informed risk, if you like. I bet on myself, on my ability, and that was the first building block to do things independently. Then the question was 'what would be my unique selling point?' With my sports and education background, I thought there was a gap that my skillset could fill...

I was head of behaviour and engagement at a school called Skinners' Academy in Hackney. It was a unique role because the headteacher believed in my ability to engage with young people. He also knew that I was a real stickler for rules and discipline and boundaries. So, when I combined those two aspects of my character, I found I did quite well.

I knew a number of the young people weren't surviving in mainstream school classes because they may have had undiagnosed additional needs. But we were sending them to local provisions that we hoped would support them to re-engage in education. But when I did some informal visits, I didn't really like the programmes that we were sending our young people to, to be honest. I used to pinch myself and say to myself, 'If I ever have the opportunity to rewrite the books, I will do it this way instead.' So you plant that seed in your head. You never think you can actually do it. Then I had the opportunity to write a programme based on my love of sport and a disciplined approach to life.

So, I visited some fantastic provisions – in Liverpool, in London – and I thought, 'I want to specialise.' I wanted to look at young people who may well be similar to how I was in school, who have a passion for sport – they love watching sport, they love participating in sport at any level – but they struggle in school. I knew that sport would be the hook and from sport they would learn so many lessons for the rest of their lives. However, some of the models that I had seen were more geared to youth work; mine, I felt, would be very different.

I wanted the young people that I worked with to be prepared for the workplace. So, we looked at recognised qualifications, and then, to give them the foundations of studying hard, they would follow high-quality personal development programmes. The Prince's Trust 'Achieve' programme and the Duke of Edinburgh Award helped build their self-esteem, developed their ability to communicate, improved their ability to work as part of a team and enabled them to show what they've done in volunteering. We established those building blocks and developed some of the skills that they didn't have in terms of being able to perform in interviews, and to be able to budget for themselves, alongside the passion and love for coaching, organising events, enterprise, etc. It gave them what they needed to study Level 3 courses post-16, such as BTECs or A-levels, or to go into a particular field that enabled them to access different sectors of sport.

What strategic support have you been able to attract?

I've been lucky enough to partner with Capita and their education department. They've been phenomenal. They've given us all our IT equipment. They're currently writing a new program specifically for us that will track and assess students. I've worked with a number of football clubs, including Crystal Palace, who've given us access to every aspect of the running of the business – the academy, the sports, science, the sports analysis, the catering, the match day team – so that the young people are looking behind the scenes, beyond what they see on TV. They suddenly realise there's a world that they can get involved in, which is also part of sport, their passion.

Combining sport with education, underpinned by high standards, became my unique selling point. I've been lucky because we are a small setting. I've recruited ex-elite sports people who have gone on to become qualified teachers. So, for example, the head of my centre is an ex-GB triple jump champion, who's also a qualified teacher. We emphasise that you can be great at sport – you can love sport – but you should also have a plan B based on educational achievement.

You developed that programme at Brent, and then you moved over to Dagenham...

I went to visit a friend at the lovely Jo Richardson School and I looked across, and there was a rugby club with beautiful playing fields. Now, I had worked at a school in Hackney, East London, on the Woodberry Down estate. It had all the social issues and challenges that you would expect. But it was a concrete jungle too – we had very little space for sport. So, I've come out to the slightly leafy suburbs and I've seen this rugby club. And I've said to myself, 'I wonder what goes on in there?' So I asked the question, and they said, 'Oh, nothing during the day,' and I went, 'Ding!'

Then I met a fantastic, incredibly inspiring headteacher, who's become my mentor, called Ges Smith, who was the headteacher of Jo Richardson School. He was retiring that year. He had an incredibly inclusive philosophy and had always wanted to run an alternative provision for the benefit of young people in the borough. I told him what I did. He came over and looked at our Brent provision, and then we explored the potential of setting up something. We met the management of the rugby club, and we decided to pilot a programme there that was a KS4 Sports Specialism.

Within three months of operation the local authority commissioned a new project. They came to me and said, 'We'd like you to start a KS3 project. You've been so successful – the schools love it, the kids are engaging, their attendance has shot up – would you like to have a look at it?' I said, 'Well, I want to cement the KS4 provision first – get our systems and structures right – but at the end of this year we will look at it.' Then the borough came to me and said, 'We've found this unique venture that we think could form a special partnership with you. They're called the OnSide. They're a group of charities and they have opened up a series of youth-based buildings. And the building in our borough is called the Future Zone – it has everything from music studios and recording studios, to climbing walls, to sports halls, to an art studio, a dance space, and an independent living suite, where you can do cooking. Basically, it had everything that you need for an SEMH specialist school, because you had purpose-built facilities for a range of activities in a fantastic new facility that was not claustrophobic. We had lots of light; in my experience, a lot of the alternative provisions were based in portacabins, hidden somewhere. Some of the most vulnerable kids that you could be working with have got some of the most horrendous facilities.

When I was building these partnerships, everyone talked to me about high-quality provision for our most vulnerable young people. And I said to myself, 'I'm eating this up all day,' because that's always what I wanted to do, the opposite of what I'd seen and did not like. I thought the most vulnerable young people should be given the *best* opportunities. So, from the conversations with parents that I had experienced about 'kicking my son out of school', the language and the narrative had become, 'Wow! You've really thought about my kid. The school has recognised that he may need some additional support. The range of activities you have – along with the brightness and the newness of this building – is fantastic.'

How important is sport to developing these young people?

Incredibly important. We do a lot of work with the Youth Sport Trust, who are trying to improve the number of hours that young people access sport.

I've engaged professional coaches who come and deliver high-quality coaching. When they first come to us, a number of kids don't understand about sharing; they don't understand about teamwork. So we use team games to teach them how to work in a team. I'll work with the weakest and talk with them about how a team is only as good as its weakest link. So, it's not all about kicking a football. We try to use the vocabulary of sport within our English lessons, within our maths lessons, which highlights our emphasis on sports throughout the academic element of our provision.

They have to be on time, or they're not participating. They have to have the right equipment, or they're not participating. They have to wear the right kit, or they're not participating. We have kit that's provided by a major sports brand, which is another way of gaining the kids' interest. They look like young sports people, and they look like they're in an elite private school. And that image, I think, is very important. It's not that you've been kicked out of mainstream. Instead, you're following your interest. You're in a place where you're going into a career of your choice.

I recently gave a talk at the Youth Sport Trust's headteachers' network. They have a theme called 'Stories', and they talk about their individual stories. And within our setup we talk about our journey. Communicating with the young people about our own struggles and challenges, and how sport has led us to this, resonates with them.

What about your KS3 provision?

We call it the Recovery programme. We identify young people who are persistently, low-level disruptive, or those who have had a string of fixed-term exclusions. They're bubbling and in danger of being permanently excluded, and we work with the schools to avoid that. We work with the most challenging kids and give them, the school and the family some time out. It's an initial six-week programme, which can be extended to 12 weeks with reviews every two weeks.

We don't want the kids to lose contact with the school, so in the first week they stay with us all five days. In the second week, they go back into their schools for one day, and we have a communication line with the school. Our mentors are sent into the schools so we can monitor how the kids are, and to ensure they don't feel they're being kicked out of school. They understand they're with us for a period of time. Our problem is making sure they understand they're going back, and they don't enjoy themselves to an extent that they think they're going to stay with us. That's why we're heavy with the academic side, and it seems to work well.

What we then do is follow them back into school to ensure they are reintegrated. That was something I learned from Skinners', where we would get the child back after, say, six weeks away in some kind of time-out centre. I wouldn't necessarily know the child was coming back and, because it was an inconvenience to me, I'd place that child in internal exclusion as a holding base. They'd have done some fantastic work for six weeks – enough for the child to re-engage in education – but because there's been a poor communication line, and I've got a lot on in a busy school of 2000 students, I've placed the child in internal exclusion and undone all that good work, and they just kick off again.

How important are maths and English?

Incredibly important. We do functional skills in KS4, which I think is important to give them a basis to work from. We talk a lot about the importance of maths and English in real life, in situations where they're going to need maths and English. A number of the young boys want to be professional footballers, and I talk with them about my first ever contract. Some of the other members of staff talk about their first ever employment contracts. The kids have no idea about the average income of jobs in any area of employment; when you present the reality, they're in actual shock. Some of them know that there are struggles at home, but they don't fully appreciate it until we have our chat.

We do an exercise where we give each young person £20. We take them to our local supermarket, and they've got to be able to feed up to three people in class with that amount of cash. That practical exercise gives them a sense of real life. We're travelling to the supermarket. We're going to buy a set of groceries, and we're going to see how much we've got left. And we're going to make that meal. So, as well as the maths, it's part of our food tech programme too. Such real-life scenarios give them a far better understanding, because the vast majority of them spend any money they are given on luxuries!

In terms of English, we take them to the professional clubs. They think the footballers just play football on a Saturday and Sunday. But when we show them that they have game analysis, where they sit in front of a screen, look at the opposition, write notes, and are tested on what they know about the opposition, it just blows their mind that even footballers have to read or write. They have to write things down if they're going to go into coaching.

I try to keep it real. We have a session we call 'Keeping it Real' where we have a very frank discussion that I may not have time to have in a mainstream school. We're realistic about things. A number of the KS4 students are at that age where they are open to the lure of county lines and gang affiliation. We encourage the young people to get a part-time job. One of the things that I've tried to do in terms of our work experience partnerships is to secure good links with community support centres and volunteering groups where we can train the young people, help them gain qualifications, support them before they go for the interview process and enable them to secure realistic paid jobs at the weekends. The kids learn about the reality of working and earning. And the hope is that they want to continue with their education, rather than be attracted by other temptations.

I read that the attendance rates are around 98%, which is phenomenal.

So, I ran a programme at Skinners' called Impact Zone. I used the school's behaviour data and identified groups who were repeat offenders in terms of behaviour but who were academically quite strong. I presented my analysis to the head and told him that I wanted to run a Saturday school. He replied, 'You're not going to get any kids in on a Saturday.'

And I said to him, 'I'm going to mix it up. I'm not going to call it maths and English. I'll call it numeracy and literacy. They'll have to do that. But I'm going to get motivational speakers, run a leadership programme, get the Arsenal community team in.'

He said, 'Okay, let's see what happens.' We selected 95 kids and 95 kids turned up... 100% attendance! We had parents' days where parents would sit in the literacy and numeracy classes. The vast majority of the kids in the school at the time were from Afro-Caribbean communities. We had Afro-Caribbean lunches to encourage the parents to come in and work with their kids. Getting parents on our side is so important.

Say a child doesn't do particularly well in school. They need to be excluded. I send the paperwork to the mainstream school. There's a start date agreed. The parents are told, and they turn up to us with the child. I do a presentation to the parents *first*, not about the child potentially having to leave that school, but about how the school fought long and hard to prevent that happening. I emphasise how they can best support their child to reach their full potential. Then the parents leave, and we bring the kids in. There's a proper induction process.

So, alongside the paper, there's a human side where we break bread with the parents at the school or do home visits. We try to build that relationship and say, 'This is a fresh start.' A lot of the parents have had poor experiences in school. But we do things slightly differently, so that they think, 'These guys are approaching me differently. They're giving me the opportunity to voice my concerns.' A lot of the parents can't access the curriculum because of language barriers. We're developing a parental programme now to see how we can best support parents to understand more about the curriculum and help their kids to be successful.

This is not dumbing down. We are a school with genuinely high expectations of the kids. And we have one adult to four students. We say to parents, 'Yes! Your child can come to a private school!' And the child–adult ratio is important. I think everyone will say this to you: *our success is based on relationships*. I hammer home to our staff the importance of developing strong relationships with the young people. I've always said it's about knowing the child and then knowing the best adult to work with that child and building those strong relationships, both with the child and with home.

You don't have to name anybody, but could you give us an example of a person who's come through your programme and has gone on to be really successful?

There are a couple of them who work for us now, which I think is one of the most fantastic success stories you could imagine! When we first met them – I'm going to be honest – they were masking low self-esteem with disruptive behaviour and sheer rudeness. They began coming in and enjoying their sports. They were given access to a range of mentors, guest speakers and visits to show them how they could follow a different path. We provided the academic and training packages, which included hands-on work experience and learning about the place of work. Then we supported them through the application process and further training for them to come back as apprentices and eventually full-time staff. They understand the young people and where they're coming from. I don't think you can beat that, if I'm honest. They are inspired and abide by our standards. If you've been in pro sport, there's no substitute for disciplined hard work. There are lines that are drawn. There's discipline.

And we celebrate every little success, even if it's the minutest thing. I take photos and videos. I send them home all the time. So, the one time I have to talk negatively to Jonny, I will have had 10 positive conversations with Mum. Then she's more likely to say to Johnny, 'Mr Dwaah supports you. He's told me 10 brilliant things about you. Come on, pick it up.' So, I also hammer home the importance of celebrating success. Let's make a big deal of any success, because a number of these kids have never had anything. They could never go on a rewards trip; they could never reach the threshold to go.

There was a troubled kid and we did a reduced timetable for him, because he just wouldn't have survived full-time. And he came in every day on the reduced timetable. I gave him a certificate. I took photos of him. He looked at me, like, 'What's up with sir?' I made it a massive deal. And you should have seen the smile on his face...

With all my colleagues I've ever worked with in alternative provision, you can feel the passion to support young people, particularly those who are less fortunate than us. I think myself very, very lucky to have the opportunity to work with some wonderful young people.

That's where the joy is

A conversation with Erin Stewart

Erin Stewart is deputy head at Glebe Farm School.

Please could you tell us about your interest in AP?

I am a governor of Active Support in Luton. I've been connected with Active Support right from the start. In 2007 we noticed a trend where pupils were doing exceptionally well in sports and PE lessons, but then they were underachieving in other subjects and having all sorts of behavioural problems. Across the school we had two incredible learning mentors in Matt Ford and Shahed Koyes. They left to set up the alternative provision and now they are the co-headteachers of Active Support.

After noticing that children were having some issues in school, initially we decided they needed some respite, but always with the sole aim of reintegrating them into mainstream. Initially, there were six-week placements. Sport was a key motivation for them. It was always about looking at where they did well, and using what they did well to manage behaviour, raise expectations to help them to achieve, and so raise their self-esteem. They were still with teachers that they knew. It was set up in the heart of the community, so it wasn't difficult for parents to get their children to and from the location, which was really important. That was really successful. The children did well, and they were able to return to school.

However, sometimes we were returning the children too quickly, before they were ready. We then extended those placements and offered a Sports Leadership qualification. That worked phenomenally well to the point where those children were then running local play clubs in the area. They were going into different schools at lunchtime, and they were running their lunchtime playground games. From that our pupils gained a very good reputation. Then the other schools asked, 'Can we refer to Active Support?' So we began to recruit from beyond our school. We started to offer a first aid course. And suddenly we were into the realms of sports coaching, and employability and longer-term placements.

And we became really popular; however, it's not a secret that some schools find themselves guilty of using alternative provision as a babysitting service for the pupils they don't have the means, resources or knowledge to cater for, and that was the reality of it, and the needs changed. We were clear that we couldn't just put a child into alternative provision with no view to reintegrate. It's not right. It's not good for them. It's also not very good for society.

So, in January 2017 we became Ofsted registered, and in 2018 we went through the first inspection to become an independent school. And that gave us school status, and we had to offer a broad and balanced curriculum almost straight away, because sport alone wasn't going to cut it. Of course, numeracy and literacy were key drivers right from the word go, and they were embedded into the routines every single day; the impact of that was massive.

And again, we had more success. We had to build a broader offer. We decided to look at four areas: construction, catering, beauty and carpentry. They were the first four in addition to the sport. We branched out into the local offer. It was like an in-house apprenticeship.

The common thread throughout our offer is leadership; the idea of empowering our children to take control of what is on offer to them in a way that can be utilised later in life. What emerged was a massive increase in self-esteem and in their application to learning. And children like learning. It's wholesome. You know, you take that small seed and you plant it, and you watch it grow. Alternative provision children are no different. You've just got to inspire them, offer them something interesting to learn. With these vocational courses you can bring that learning to life. That's where the fun is. That's where the joy is.

However, when it's an alternative provision you can't be naive. A child coming into alternative provision is going to have vulnerabilities, and the core vulnerabilities that we saw were low-level numeracy, low-level literacy and PSHE. You have to have something really interesting that they want to do. We are now looking at how we're going to introduce phonics schemes into our alternative provision, and we're looking for creative ways to expand our reading offer. Our numeracy course looks at financial management, tying it in with business and enterprise. We are always looking to link with our unifying theme of leadership for life.

Active Support is located right next to a place called Venue Central that is running all of our catering and hospitality events. We have a gym on site for when we're offering some of the sport. The contractors have a downstairs floor where students learn carpentry; everything else takes place on site. They're not actually travelling out. We are a big alternative provision but we are a school. We feel like a school. We're not sticking students on a bus and sending them 20 miles away to go do whatever it is and then come back because you're detached from it.

Construction, catering, beauty and carpentry weren't just plucked from the air. They mirror the KS5 offer at the local college, because once they finish with us they can progress to the college. Leadership and enterprise run through everything, and what makes it innovative is that we apply social media, marketing, employability, business practice and financial management to each of those four vocational areas. If you are studying construction, you're going to look at how to set up your own construction company. When we're looking at catering, you're going to learn how to run a restaurant. If it's beauty, are you working independently or working as part of a team? Are you going to be a franchise?

Beyond the enterprise and employability skills, the careers offer is also about offering work experience. The stigma around being able to offer a work experience placement to a student in an alternative provision is so difficult to get around because of society's negative view of children in alternative provision. We've got to change that perception. Children love learning. Children love achieving. You know that once they've got that self-esteem, the world is their oyster, it really is. So, Venue Central is right next door. It's a huge wedding venue, really, where you can host various different events, but the children from Active Support will be waiters and waitresses. They'll work in the kitchens. Many are given summer jobs. When you think about the loyalty to the alternative provision, these students suddenly say, 'Hang on a minute. I've got a sustainable, wonderful income. I love this place. I want to be in this place.'

We then added boxing to our curriculum, mainly due to Kay Prosper, who is a European boxing champion from Luton and a local hero, choosing to operate out of our gym. Boys and girls both do boxing, and we emphasise the fitness aspect of the sport. We didn't want to lose sight of our roots; while we talk about business and enterprise, leadership and entrepreneurship, we are aware that our core business – sports and teamwork, physical and mental health, wellbeing, all of that – was where we began.

So, all of this fantastic stuff was happening with all of these incredible things that were taking place and then bang! The pandemic hit. When they came back to the alternative provision, the students were so different. And our curriculum had to adapt accordingly. They came back with much lower resilience. They came back with a need for instant gratification from anything that they were doing, but there was also the need for tangible results and safety to fail. They needed to see their learning taking place physically. So, we offered things like pottery, barbering, jewellery, things where you get tangible success: 'Oh, my goodness! I've just made that! I've just created that!' We had to restructure the day as the projects were bite-size to keep the students interested.

The students needed a reason to get up. If they were punctual in the morning for the literacy and numeracy, then in the afternoon they were rewarded with what they would like to do. So, if a student wanted to go in the gym, fine, let's do an hour in the gym and complete these three tasks. Such an approach really did help, but it also ensured that our students became the protagonists in their own stories. They chose what they pursued. We said, 'Your learning is so important to us that we trust you to make good choices. Look what good things happen when you are championing yourself.' It's incredibly flexible. If there are three members of staff, we'll say, 'Right, we're going to offer the gym. We're going to offer the baking, and we're going to offer hospitality,' and then the students can choose from those three activities.

Are students there because they've been permanently excluded as an intervention?

There is, of course, the therapeutic side of what we do. There have been times where circumstances outside of anyone's control mean that the child needs to have a period of time away from school. Now, if it's a short period of time, we will facilitate online learning with some of our schools using Google Classroom. They can still study and submit their work. We do insist on regular live teacher check-ins. And the teachers spend half an hour of their time talking through the work, both with the child and with a member of our staff. I think it's worth noting that we facilitate teacher training at Active Support, which is something unusual in AP. Our lead trainer Louise Stewart facilitates all our teacher training, and she's also a qualified SENDCO.

How have you sustained the leadership strand?

So, where are the opportunities for them to lead in sport? Well, of course, refereeing, for instance. We put them through the qualifications for refereeing. We'll take them to a football game. They can see the role of the referee in context. Or they will lead the warm-up before a PE lesson. Or they might lead a training session. We insist that they apply the leadership knowledge that they've gained. What does leadership look like in catering? If you're running a restaurant, how many staff do you need? What does each person do? How much are you going to pay them? If this is how much you need to make, how much do you need to charge for a meal? What about sourcing the ingredients? And they think about things like the aesthetics, and how they would promote their restaurant on social media. And we say, 'If you were the CEO, what would you do? You know, you're the decision maker. You're the one who decides.' That's where that energy and creativity and ambition come from. They're inspired by what they're doing. In science we bombard them with practicals, every single lesson... practical, practical, practical, practical. When the students are reintegrated into their home schools, and they are taking science qualifications, they find their grades have gone through the roof. And the reason for that is because they're inspired. They now love what they're doing. If you love what you're doing, you'll never work again.

Leadership is closely linked to empowerment and self-esteem. There's a piece of research on safeguarding that says the 'don't carry knives, save lives' approach to youth crime is ineffective. Pointing out what the law says, and saying this is what you must do and must not do, has no impact on some young people. Knife crime is rooted in a lack of self-esteem and being unable to see a future beyond anything that's immediately ahead of you. And that's how they feel. You can tell them the law. They know that they're still going to break it. You can tell them that if they carry a knife they're more likely to be stabbed because of it. They know that. But until you make children feel good about themselves and feel that there's hope for a positive future, nothing will change behaviours. That's what an alternative provision should do – provide a fresh start and hope for something better.

What we keep saying to our children is that your outcome is not just your results. Your results are a result of everything else. The actual end product is *you*; a happy, safe, functioning, contributing member of society.

We can talk about the safeguarding curriculum. We can talk about PSHE, but I think fundamentally it comes down to taking the time to really understand your learners. It's about relationships. They are everything – every single thing. And it's the same in life. You take the time to really get to know these children, their passions, their skills, their talents, their love. That's where you start. And they can move mountains. Yes, they have vulnerabilities, and yes, they are overcoming some tremendous struggles. But these children are full of potential and all it takes is time to really get to know and understand them.

Teach Me Happy

A conversation with Adele Lord-Laverick and Georgina Gowthorpe

Adele Lord-Laverick and Georgina Gowthorpe are co-founders of Teach Me Happy, an independent alternative provision in York.

Tell us a bit about the history of Teach Me Happy.

Adele Lord-Laverick (AL-L): Myself and Gorgi started teaching together seven years ago – we trained as primary school teachers in the East Riding at the same school. Both of my children have special educational needs. My son is autistic and dyspraxic and my daughter is dyslexic, autistic and has ADHD and auditory processing disorder. When you have children and you're a teacher, you know what you want to offer pupils as a teacher, but you also know as a parent what your child needs in the classroom. I am also just completing my doctorate in autism research.

Gorgi Gowthorpe (GG): Adele and I have always had an interest in special educational needs. I went on to become the SENDCO of our primary school. Throughout my life my parents have fostered, and through that I've seen and experienced a lot of childhood trauma and seen the special needs that the children have struggled with in the classroom.

AL-L: We'd always said, 'We'll have our own provision one day.' We were talking just before the school holidays in 2022, and we just said, 'You know what? Let's do it. We're in the best place professionally and personally to start something.' There was very little alternative provision for primary-aged children as most of the provision was for secondary. We found that lots of provision didn't have qualified teaching staff, and we're very passionate about children with SEND having the same quality of education that all children have, whether they're in a mainstream classroom or not. My own children were occasionally refusing to go to school, and I understand how much pressure that puts on parents. So, basically, we went out and we found a building. Two weeks later we had the building, and then we spent the next six months creating our provision, before our opening in January 2023.

So, Adele, was it born out of your experience? Was that a driving force for you?

AL-L: Yes, I think so. My son always achieved very good marks, had no outward behaviours, but he would be very emotional and upset when he came home. The teaching staff couldn't see the struggles that he was having. But at home we'd see that 'Coke bottle explosion' you'll hear lots of people talk about. I understand as a teacher that when we have children in the classroom, we don't see their needs that are seen only at home. Teachers can't really report on needs they don't see. It means there often isn't enough evidence to get diagnoses or apply for an EHCP to secure the funding that you need for specialist provision. I began to see the issue from every point of view. I started my doctorate of education, interviewing parents and professionals within the referral process. I saw how everybody has barriers: teachers, SENDCOs, parents. Nothing really worked. I was driven. I wanted to know what I could do as a person to improve things, to help my children, teachers and parents. I wanted to know how we could work together to provide a better experience for our children.

What were the principles behind the way you planned your provision?

GG: High-quality teaching was one of the main principles. We wanted a welcoming space. We wanted something that was very open, very spacious. We wanted to look out of beautiful windows at beautiful surroundings; a very calming environment. We wanted to build those trusting relationships that would enable children to learn. Our initial priority is for children to be emotionally well. When children are emotionally well, they will be able to learn. And that's what we really wanted to provide.

We also wanted to provide a space for our parents. When you're a parent of a child with additional needs, it can feel very isolating. We wanted something where parents could come together, speak to one another, find their own ways through the system and *lean* on each other, to know they are not alone. That was a big drive for us as well. So having somewhere where parents can come to and where they've got people that are with them in their journey was really important to us.

So, you've got the children emotionally in a good space. You've got parents trusting you. You've got a gorgeous building. What did you decide to teach them?

AL-L: We have the national curriculum, which is an excellent foundation for all learning. We went through all the subjects on the national curriculum and started to group/connect them, and we designed learning activities to help the pupils learn. For instance, if you're studying the Romans, rather than have a PowerPoint for the lesson in the classroom, and then a little task, we'll go out. We'll visit a Roman well, we'll look at a medieval castle, we'll walk around the Shambles and investigate things. We do things from a very practical angle, so that the children have that full, sensory approach to learning. And then Gorgi and I spend lots of time taking pictures and making observations, so that we have evidence of what they've learned.

Gorgi's story is so important, because we do have looked-after children in the provision, and part of our provision is Gorgi's family home, which is her farm with stables. I'll let you talk about that, Gorgi.

GG: So, my parents have been foster carers for a very long time. They offer equine therapy, which is when the children spend the time with the animals, and nobody's judging them. They learn so much about horses. 'Okay, let's have a look at what brushes we've got here, and what parts of the horse we need to brush with which brush.' And it's about being outside. It's the fresh air, and it's giving them that time to go and regulate. They might have had a bad day at school, and then they just won't really speak when they get home. But then they go out with the horses. We'll feed them. We'll look after them and you'll just find the children in the stable with one of the horses, and they'll be talking about the day. It's about letting them have a bit of time to regulate themselves, and unfortunately they just don't get that in a mainstream school. Developing speaking and listening, and being in that outside environment, all threads back into mainstream provision for the children who are in split settings.

The teachers have said what a massive impact that's had on the children. Some of the foster children have followed careers linked with animals or with horses specifically. It's given them a passion and something they feel they're good at. And their self-esteem has risen through that. And it is unbelievable. And we've had parents who say that their children have now got a passion and interest, and how they've got something outside of school and education that they think they're good at.

AL-L: Gorgi's mum and dad still have foster children. It's just their awareness of the importance of reassuring a looked-after child that they're not on their own. It's not just them. They're not isolated. I guess that feeling of community is key for all of us. We really celebrate special educational needs; one of the children in the classroom last week said, 'Put your hand up if you're autistic. Yay!' and it is just a really great thing for them.

You've got the therapeutic element of being with the horses, which develops children's oracy, which could also be internal – it's not just the voice that comes out, but the voice within. And then there's being involved with the brushing and feeding, which develops their ability to follow instructions. These are all the kinds of things that you would have in a regular classroom but actually it's in a living, breathing space. It's just such a rich thing that you have described. I'd be interested in the extent to which there's intersectionality between young people there with SEND, and your provision of an alternative provision. So how do you frame your offer to schools and local authorities? Are you offering a special educational needs alternative provision?

AL-L: We offer alternative provision. That said, we find that many of our children do have special educational needs, because they struggle in the classroom. But we offer alternative provision. We offer up to 13 hours of education a week, which is obviously well within the legal framework for an AP. We offer both primary and secondary education but separate our primary and secondary days, and for our secondary days we're now offering top-up tutoring. We do after-school tutoring, which is attached to the stable. We also were gifted a paddock by Gorgi's mum and dad, and that's been kindly developed by Network Rail. They've built an outdoor classroom and polytunnel, and they set up some raised beds. So now they've got this huge space where we could teach them gardening-based activities. We aren't very good at gardening, but we manage some big groups and a couple of tomato plants! It was the best thing we'd ever done. We even got a courgette! I mean, these are life skills for us!

Genius, it's genius, Gorgi! So how are these places funded? Are they through the local authority? Are they through schools? How does it work?

GG: We run like a council-run enhanced provision. A lot of our pupils are schooled in split settings. They remain in mainstream, and they come to us as well. Some schools will fund places from the EHCP top-up funding for the individual child. We have some children who don't have EHCPs, so they take that from the SEND budget. We've got some pupils who are home-schooled, so parents will pay for those places themselves. We've got some children who have applied through local charities to get a place with us. And now we've offered our first subsidised place; this is where we feel that we could help a student in genuine need. We're basically offering free places that we pay for out of the funds that we've raised from the children who come into the setting. All that we earn goes back into the business. We recently bought a minibus so that we can transport more children to the farm for horse therapy.

It's just quite remarkable. I'm blown away by it. Amazing! Gosh! How many children and how many staff do you have currently?

AL-L: We offer support for over 50 children now across the week, and we have employed four new members of staff, all of whom are qualified teachers or teaching assistants. Our latest recruit has been working with looked-after children in social care for a long time, so we feel that she will have the skills needed to look after those children who are really the most vulnerable in our society.

You mentioned that you've got a secondary provision. What do you teach them? What qualifications do they get? What's the relationship with mainstream?

AL-L: Monday is primary. In the morning we offer maths and English, but we also focus on a subject per week. So it might be history week, for example. So all of our units of work might be threaded through Romans, or something like that, all within the national curriculum. And then in the afternoon we go to the farm. So Gorgi is obviously a horse specialist and she's a show jumper. She's just completed a show jumping coaching training qualification. So Gorgi will be doing things for the horses, and I'll be teaching gardening – lots of holistic activities such as digging our own path, and we're going to learn how to pave a stone path.

Tuesdays are secondary. In the morning, we study maths, English and science in 20-minute lessons. We're not the main educator, but for children who aren't in school we're providing top-up tutoring. We focus on bridging the gaps for children who have been out of school for a long time. We assess them, and because we're trained, qualified primary school teachers, we know what they need foundationally to be successful later on, and we focus on filling those learning gaps. In the afternoons we go to the farm. We have recently become a functional skills centre, so we offer functional skills maths and English, which are equivalent to GCSEs.

Wednesdays are for primary, so they look the same as the Mondays. Our Thursdays are secondary, but they're mainly for children on the autism spectrum who have high anxiety. They are children who can't get in to school. It's all about building up their confidence and getting them into groups. So, Gorgi heads with a group to the farm in the morning with another teacher. I stay at the provision and do holistic activities and really focus on developing social and communication skills. And then we swap the groups so that we keep small group sizes, and they get the best of both worlds. And then on a Friday Gorgi takes the secondary. I keep the primary and then we swap them over in the afternoon. It just evolves over time. We're always thinking of different ways in which we can get the most out of what we do. So, will it look like this in six months? Probably not.

GG: We offer functional skills because for some of our pupils we don't think GCSEs are suitable. We are looking at how we can help them be more employable or how to get onto an apprenticeship. We're evolving all the time.

AL-L: We can now also deliver life skills where students learn about managing their money and going to interviews – skills that will help them beyond their time with us.

It's so interesting. You reject entirely the deficit model of working with these children. You look at what they can do, rather than get vexed about what they can't do. It's just so refreshing. It's about celebrating achievement and making sure they get a certificate – recognition that they've been successful – because they've had a life up to this point of not being successful.

AL-L: Yes, we get that a lot from parents when we ring them up and say, 'Oh, hi! It's Teach Me Happy. (They always think there is a problem...) Oh, no, no! We're ringing you to tell you how kind they've been... We're ringing to tell you how resilient they've been,' and the parents say, 'Oh, my goodness! You know, I haven't had a phone call like this in years.' All the certificates that we offer through IXL (an online learning platform) are sent straight to parents, and one parent said, 'That's the first certificate that my child has ever had, thank you so much.' IXL breaks things down into really small chunks. Some of our children can only learn for two minutes – that's their limit. But if we can sit them down and teach them for two minutes, then they've done something more than they would have been doing. And then the teachers in their mainstream school can see that on IXL and the parents can see that too. We've had some schools that have bought into IXL so that they can deliver the same kind of package that we deliver at Teach Me Happy.

So that synergy between you and the mainstream schools is strong, is it? How does that work?

GG: We do have an online platform that's linked between parents and teachers. Any progress or any achievements or photos, observations, and anything that we've scribed all goes on to that drive every session. So mainstream school staff and the parents can all look at that, and then they can talk about the day with that particular pupil. One of our main aims is to get pupils back into a mainstream setting. So, we encourage mainstream staff to come into our provision as that first step to building that relationship with teachers and help the children back into school.

AL-L: We've said from the beginning, 'What do the children need from us? What do they want from us? How are we going to make this successful?' Sometimes, we spend hours planning this fantastic week, and the children come in and we say that they can't learn today because they're not emotionally ready. And so we do something different. Our children often need something quite different.

Just to finish... About your parents, Gorgi, how fantastic that they've been involved. It's just beautiful.

GG: Yes, we're really lucky – really, really lucky. It's something that is a little bit different. My parents are incredible people. I don't know many other parents who would want 50 children coming onto their property! But that is their passion. They've helped a lot of children over the years. They are long-term foster carers; one child was five when they came to us, and they're 19 now. They still live with us. My parents are in it for the long haul. As soon as me and my sister moved out, our bedrooms were full! They've got four foster children at the moment. My mum says she just wants to make a difference to the greatest number of children possible, and if she can do that through Teach Me Happy as well as through her fostering, everyone benefits. She likes to get all of them a drink and a snack when they leave. It's like a little tuck shop. She says that it brings her a little bit of joy in the day to give them a treat after their day with us.

A sense of freedom

A conversation with Izzy and Sara

Izzy is 16 years old. She has been home educated, largely by her mum Sara, since Year 3.

So, Izzy is now 16 and she has been home educated since she was eight years old. It would be good to talk through how you made that decision and then what you've studied since being home educated for the last eight years.

Sara: I've always been interested in home education. We've got two children, and before they started school, home education was something I'd looked into. But we found a school that we liked and applied, and both girls started school, but Izzy never really took to it. Reception was okay, but in Years 1 and 2 Izzy wasn't keen. She didn't want to go, but we pushed through. But by Year 3, Izzy was really, really not happy. She was unwell. A lot of the time she was very stressed and wasn't learning well. We engaged with the school, and it gave us some strategies to help. Izzy just survived school, but I really wanted an environment for her to thrive in. I didn't want to just help her get through it. I didn't want that to be her childhood. I wanted her to thrive because she's really bright, and she was a huge character as a small child, and that was dripping away from her through the stress. I'd suggested quite a few times to the school that Izzy was probably dyslexic, as I am, and that wasn't really looked into, so

223

she never really got the support she needed to enable her to learn. And then she had a bit of a cold, and she said, 'I can't go to school. I'm ill.' I said, 'You do need to go to school. You can't stay off because you've got a bit of a cold.' And she said to me, 'Mum, it takes everything I've got to get through the day. I can't do it if I'm not feeling 100%.' And that was a real moment when I said, 'Oh, hang on a minute. This really isn't okay.' And she didn't go back after that day.

What was that moment like, Izzy?

Izzy: I don't really remember most of my school years to be honest, but I do remember that sense of relief when my parents finally said, 'Right, we get it. You don't have to go back.' My mum said, 'If you want to go back for one more day to say bye to your friends, you can.' And I said, 'I never want to step foot in that building again. No, thank you.'

So, you've made that tumultuous decision. What happened next?

Sara: I was most concerned about Izzy being okay, because she was still fairly young. I didn't feel huge amounts of pressure academically. And so I said to Izzy, 'Right, what would you like to learn about?' And she said, 'Chocolate and poo!' A seven-year-old's answer! So, we did. We learned about the digestive system, and we went to Eureka (the National Children's Museum) and did the 'Mouth to Poo' experience. We did experiments to do with the digestive system. We did chocolate tasting and learned about percentages of cacao. And we did surveys and made graphs. And it was amazing! We looked at Africa, where they grow a lot of the cacao, and then we made tie-dye clothes and African stew, and we got an African drummer to come to see us. It was incredible how these first ideas from Izzy sparked her learning. We contacted someone from the church who'd worked for Christian Aid and been to Africa. We reached out. We learned organically, especially in the early days.

Was it trial and error in those early days?

Sara: Yes, looking back on it. We also really prioritised meeting other home-ed families. I knew other people who home educated, which I think really helped the decision. Straight away we were in a community. We did things with other home-educated children straight away. I remember one of the friends was really into snails, so we did snail racing and measured how far the snails got in a certain amount of time and baked snail biscuits and made mosaic snail art. We would pick up on any of the kids' interests and go with it.

You would follow those threads across the curriculum – you had a bit of science, a bit of maths, a bit of English, all woven together just through your creativity, Izzy.

Izzy: Yeah. I do remember bits of those earlier days. I remember my first day being home-schooled because my parents weren't expecting it. My mum had work to go to, and my dad was going on a fishing trip with his dad. So on my first day being home educated, I went on a fishing trip with my dad and my granddad. And that was a lot of fun. And that was like my main memory from those early days.

How was it socially for you at that time? What about your school friends – how did that work?

Izzy: It was really good. I wasn't in as much contact with my school friends as before, but I still saw them occasionally. I made lots of new friends in home-ed, and because of our age, everyone was just friends with everyone, because we all just wanted to play games, and our parents were good at engaging us in different activities and combining all our interests together. So, I feel like my social life was really good.

That's great. So, when did it get slightly more formal? Because you get to the end of primary... Was there a transition moment? Did it get more formal before you got to the end of Year 6? Or were you just educating organically all the way up until that point?

Sara: It was a very gradual transition. There was no big change at that point. I mean, our experience was really punctuated by COVID. Izzy was 12 when COVID hit, so I'd say up until that point it was super organic – a lot done in big groups. We had a lot of friends, and actually she spent most of the time playing. She just played and played and played and played and played. We'd get together for Science Group, and we'd get into little groups and they'd do an activity that maybe would take a certain amount time, and then they'd spend four hours playing, which, for me, was one of the absolute benefits of home-educating – just being able to do what kids naturally want to do.

And did you have any guidance from a national curriculum book that said what you should cover?

Sara: I didn't buy the national curriculum book, but I found it online. To be honest, I clicked through it. But it did make me think, 'Oh, yeah, let's think about this and that.' But I wasn't at all fussed about following the national curriculum, and I really wanted Izzy to experience things and have the opportunity to follow her interests. So, we went to all the museums possible. We went to Liverpool. We went to Newcastle. We went to all of York's amazing sites. We've been on Tesco Tours. We've been to the Amazon distribution centre. We've been to the power station. We've been where our rubbish gets recycled and the Buddhist centre. It was really about getting out and about and engaging with what's on offer. I really enjoyed science, so we joined a science group, and we actually created our own science group in the end, and we would bring the kids together to study science.

I really didn't want her experiences to be limited by home-ed. I was more interested in her being exposed to things rather than the key details of a curriculum that didn't feel that important. It felt more important that she could access information, learn new scientific language and knew how to think critically. We worked a lot on skills rather than specific information. And she started a Maths Games Group, which was really lovely. You loved that, didn't you Izzy? And then she was diagnosed with dyslexia through a private test, and the educational psychologist recommended 'Beat Dyslexia', which was a quite a structured literacy programme that I worked on with Izzy. She also had another tutor, one-on-one, for numeracy and literacy.

Izzy: I had an English tutor pretty much from the beginning of school at Year 1, and just kept seeing her. She still tutors me now as my English teacher.

Sara: I think you were six or seven when you were struggling at school, and I thought maybe a tutor would help, and so she actually did maths and English with you for a long time, and just does English now. And so there's always a bit more structure to the maths and English.

That would make sense. So, COVID hit, and then everybody was at home. And you would have been Year 7 age then, Izzy. How are you feeling at that point as you moved into the secondary age?

Izzy: To be honest, I was just quite happy. I had lots of time with my animals, which is my main thing. And despite COVID, I could still ride horses and be around animals, because that was allowed. I had a friend who was at the yard quite a lot, so we'd just hang out together at the yard, socially distanced, and go on hacks together. And it was a good time. I had my tutors, which moved to online. I was learning online as well as starting a few programmes like the Prince's Trust.

Sara: It was quite a positive time for us. We had a lot of family time, didn't we? Things did change at that point because we weren't going to the museums, and we weren't doing the group meet-ups. That was probably when the more formal school stuff set in.

What were you learning then?

Sara: You did foundation level in the British Horse Society qualification. And she was carrying on with the maths and English. We did gardening. We grew vegetables, and I also bought the only curriculum I have ever bought. It's called the Nature Curriculum. It's a nature journal that guides you as a gardener throughout the year and so we dipped into that.

Izzy: And there was the science thing you bought...

Sara: Yeah, we did try doing science. I did that for a good few months before we gave up. We tried the biology GCSE. I love biology. I did a health studies degree. It was so hard! But it was really enjoyable learning about biology again. But what I know from my other daughter who is at school full-time is that you have to memorise it word for word to pass the exam. It's not about having an understanding of the subject.

Izzy: It was just getting a bit painful. One of the reasons we stopped was that I didn't need a science GCSE to get into the college I want to go to. I only need maths and English, so it seems silly to be working towards science too when I'm not the most academic person. I thought I could put more of my time and energy into focusing on things I would need for my future. So, we do lots of reading. We read. I do like reading.

Sara, were you reading too?

Sara: Yeah, we always incorporated a lot of reading and made it fun. Izzy wasn't good at sitting still! We had a squishy that we used as a bookmark. When I read to her when she was younger, she'd usually be hanging upside down with a squishy.

Izzy: Then reading clicked in. I still really like those children's books because they engage my brain. I like those ones the most, which is maybe a bit childish.

All reading's good reading, as far as I'm concerned! What are your thoughts about taking any examinations?

Izzy: I'm going to take my maths and English exams, because I want to go to Askham Bryan College and I need a grade 4 in both maths and English.

How are you prepping for those exams?

Izzy: For four days a week I have tutors and they set me homework too. And other various, you know, activities I have like The Prince's Trust, which is the equivalent of two GCSEs.

How do you see your future once you finish college? What would you love to be doing when you wake up on your 19th birthday?

Izzy: My ideal thing would be to work with horses or animals. I'd love to be a horse-riding instructor, even though it's a tough job, and it's a cold job in the winter. It's just my ideal thing to do, being able to be around animals all day and meet lots of interesting people, and just follow my passion.

That sounds great! And good to hear you know what it entails! Let me finish with this question: what are the three best pieces of advice for anybody thinking about home-educating?

Sara: Well, firstly, I would say have a period of de-schooling, because you and your child will need time to recover, especially if you have taken a child out of school because it's not working. Your child needs some time to recover, and as a parent you need some time to just let go of the school system. Izzy quite often does her work in the evening now, because she's a teenager. She has more energy than she does in the morning. You can go with the flow a lot more.

You have to let go of what you think education looks like. A child doesn't necessarily need to be sat at a desk with a book to be learning. So, I think that period of de-schooling is really important.

That's so interesting. That's a great first one... Two more.

Sara: Oh, I never, ever let anything affect my relationship with Izzy. I don't think that we have ever fallen out over schoolwork...

Izzy: There was that maths thing you tried to get me to do... It was just proper school stuff! I had to sit in a classroom with loads of other children, and I just had to sit silently for an hour. And I hate sitting still, especially silently. There was nothing interactive. There were no animals, nothing that interested me. And that was not fun!

Sara: I had forgotten that! But, yeah, relationship comes first. We don't fall out. If we did let the schoolwork make us fall out, I think that would be awful. I am not the teacher. We don't have that sort of relationship. I'm a facilitator of Izzy's learning. If you're going to fall out, you may as well be in school. Home has to be a safe place, doesn't it?

And a third tip?

Sara: Get involved with the home-education community and make connections. I couldn't imagine doing it without that. That's been, I would say, for both of us, 100% essential. You're part of a community, just not a *school* community. It's a home-education community. We still do lots of stuff! We've been ice skating, and we've been to the escape rooms as part of youth group every week. So even as a normal teenager, it's still really, really important to our home-ed experience. (To Izzy) Have you got any tips?

Izzy: Just don't worry about it. I was worried that I wasn't going to have any friends, and that it was going to get weird. When people were speaking to me, I would say that I was home educated. I thought people were going to think that's really weird. But nobody actually cares. So, just do what feels right for you.

It's an easy, stereotypical view of you just being at home on your own wading through textbooks from school... Instead it sounds like it's a very liberal and enlightened approach to educating someone.

Sara: I think the key to it is that it's what you want it to be. And of all the home-educators we know, no one does it exactly like we do it. The key for me was creating something that was completely bespoke to Izzy, and it's utterly changeable. We have full control over it, so if we need to pull back because we're a bit under the weather, that's fine. We do a little bit less or, if Izzy suddenly sparks an interest in geology, we find a geologist, and they come and teach us through the power of chocolate about rocks!

You know it's a massive task to take on. It's been expensive for us, and it has been a huge commitment, I'd say, on my part. Luckily, I have loved it. I've thrived while doing it. But it's not something to be taken on lightly. In terms of an education, it would be hard to find something that suited the individual child better, because you create it on a day-to-day basis to suit your child.

You don't necessarily need a curriculum. You need the imagination and creativity to build upon what your child wants to learn about. And you also need to be able to afford to home-educate. I know that not everyone has a mum who could stop work like I could. The mixture of age groups is great and they teach each other. The sense of freedom is the overwhelming benefit.

Well, you both seem unbelievably happy! Thank you so much.